D1318900

JIM
CARREY

JIM
CARREY

Mary Hughes

Introduction by James Scott Brady,
Trustee, the Center to Prevent Handgun Violence
Vice Chairman, the Brain Injury Foundation

Chelsea House Publishers
Philadelphia

CHELSEA HOUSE PUBLISHERS

EDITOR IN CHIEF Stephen Reginald
PRODUCTION MANAGER Pamela Loos
MANAGING EDITOR James D. Gallagher
PICTURE EDITOR Judy L. Hasday
ART DIRECTOR Sara Davis
SENIOR PRODUCTION EDITOR Lisa Chippendale

Staff for **Jim Carrey**
SENIOR EDITOR Therese De Angelis
ASSOCIATE ART DIRECTOR Takeshi Takahashi
DESIGNER Brian Wible
PICTURE RESEARCHER Patricia Burns
COVER ILLUSTRATOR Steve Brodner

3 5 7 9 8 6 4 2

Library of Congress Cataloging-in-Publication Data

Hughes, Mary.
Jim Carrey / by Mary Hughes.
102 pp. cm. — (Overcoming adversity)
Includes bibliographical references and index.
Summary: Describes the personal life and professional career of the
comedian who has starred in such movies as "The Mask," "The Cable
Guy," and "Batman Forever."
ISBN 0-7910-4698-2 (hc)
1. Carrey, Jim, 1962- —Juvenile literature. 2. Comedians—United
States—Biography—Juvenile Literature. 3. Motion picture actors and
actresses—United States—Biography—Juvenile Literature. [1. Carrey,
Jim, 1962- . 2. Comedians. 3. Actors and Actresses.]
I. Title. II. Series.
PN2287.C278H84 1998
791.43'028'092—dc21
[B]   97-51396
                                                              CIP
                                                               AC

Frontis: *Jim Carrey
receives a "kiss" from
his canine costar of*
The Mask.

CONTENTS

OVERCOMING ADVERSITY

TIM ALLEN
comedian/performer

MAYA ANGELOU
author

APOLLO 13 MISSION

DREW BARRYMORE
actress

DREW CAREY
comedian/performer

JIM CARREY
comedian/performer

BILL CLINTON
U.S. President

TOM CRUISE
actor

MICHAEL J. FOX
actor

WHOOPI GOLDBERG
comedian/performer

EKATERINA GORDEEVA
figure skater

SCOTT HAMILTON
figure skater

JAMES EARL JONES
actor

QUINCY JONES
composer

ABRAHAM LINCOLN
U.S. President

WILLIAM PENN
Pennsylvania's founder

ROSEANNE
entertainer

SAMMY SOSA
baseball player

DAVE THOMAS
entrepreneur

ROBIN WILLIAMS
comedian/performer

ON FACING ADVERSITY

James Scott Brady

I GUESS IT'S a long way from a Centralia, Illinois, train yard to the George Washington University Hospital Trauma Unit. My dad was a yardmaster for the old Chicago, Burlington & Quincy Railroad. As a child, I used to get to sit in the engineer's lap and imagine what it was like to drive that train. I guess I always have liked being in the "driver's seat."

Years later, however, my interest turned from driving trains to driving campaigns. In 1979, former Texas governor John Connally hired me as a press secretary in his campaign for the American presidency. We lost the Republican primary to a former Hollywood star named Ronald Reagan. But I managed to jump over to the Reagan campaign. When Reagan was elected in 1980, I was "sitting in the catbird seat," as humorist James Thurber would say—poised to be named presidential press secretary. I held that title throughout the eight years of the Reagan administration. But not without one terrible, extended interruption.

It happened barely two months after the Reagan administration took office. I never even heard the shots. On March 30, 1981, my life went blank in an instant. In an attempt to assassinate President Reagan, John Hinckley Jr. armed himself with a "Saturday Night Special"—a low quality, $29 pistol—and shot wildly as our presidential entourage exited a Washington hotel. One of the exploding bullets struck me just above the left eye. It shattered into a couple dozen fragments, some of which penetrated my skull and entered my brain.

The next few months of my life were a nightmare of repeated surgery, broken contact with the outside world, and a variety of medical complications. More than once, I was very close to death.

The next few years were filled with frustrating struggles to function with a paralyzed right side, struggles to speak and communicate.

To people who face and defeat daunting obstacles, "ambition" is not becoming wealthy or famous or winning elections or awards. Words like "ambition" and "achievement" and "success" take on very different meanings. The objective is just to live, to wake up every morning. The goals are not lofty; they are very ordinary.

My own heroes are ordinary folks—but they accomplish extraordinary things because they try. My greatest hero is my wife, Sarah. She's accomplished a lot of things in life, but two stand out. The first has been the way she has cared for me and our son since I was shot. A tremendous tragedy and burden was dropped unexpectedly into her life, totally beyond her control and without justification. She could have given up; instead, she focused her energies on preserving our family and returning our lives to normal as much as possible. Week by week, month by month, year by year, she has not reached for the miraculous, just for the normal. Yet in focusing on the normal, she has helped accomplish the miraculous.

Her other most remarkable accomplishment, to me, has been spearheading the effort to keep guns out of the hands of criminals and children in America. Opponents call her a "gun grabber"; I call her a national hero. And I am not alone.

After a seven-year battle, during which Sarah and I worked tirelessly to educate the public about the need for stronger gun laws, the Brady Bill became law in 1993. It was a victory, achieved in the face of tremendous opposition, that now benefits all Americans. Since the law has been in effect, background checks have stopped 173,000 criminals and other high-risk purchasers from buying handguns, and the law has helped to reduce illegal gun trafficking.

Sarah was not pursuing fame, or even recognition. She simply started at one point—when our son, Scott, found a loaded handgun on the seat of a pickup truck and, thinking it was a toy, pointed it at Sarah. Fortunately, no one was hurt. But seeing a gun nearly bring a second tragedy upon our family, Sarah became determined to do whatever she could to prevent senseless death and injury from guns.

Some people think of Sarah as a powerful political force. To me, she's the person who so many times fed me and helped me dress during my long years of recovery.

Overcoming obstacles is part of life, not just for people who are challenged by disabilities, illnesses, or tragedies, but for all people. No matter what the obstacle—fear, disability, prejudice, grief, or a difficulty that isn't likely to "just go away"—we can all work to make this world a better place.

Jim Carrey as the offbeat sleuth who tracks a kidnapped Super Bowl quarterback in Ace Ventura, Pet Detective.

1

BIG AT THE
BOX OFFICE

AS THE MOVIE *Ace Ventura, Pet Detective* was opening in Atlanta, Georgia, its star was busy cruising the streets of the city, driving from theater to theater, looking to see if his name was really up on the marquees. Jim Carrey wasn't completely convinced that his name would be there. He had to see it for himself. He had called his friend Wayne Flemming and asked him to come to Atlanta that weekend in February of 1994, for the express purpose of checking out movie marquees.

Carrey and Flemming had known each other a long time. Both started out on the Canadian comedy circuit as stand-up comedians. A 17-year-old Jim Carrey had once counted on Wayne Flemming to give him a ride home from a comedy club in Toronto, Ontario. Now he believed that he could count on Flemming to help him get through this nerve-wracking weekend.

Carrey was right. Flemming came to Atlanta, prepared to read as many marquees as necessary. He understood how his buddy felt. Jim needed a little help convincing himself that his fame was real. Seeing his name on movie marquees would give Jim some visible proof that he really had received star billing in a nationally distributed movie.

As it turned out, Carrey had absolutely nothing to worry about. There it was—JIM CARREY—spelled out correctly on the theater marquees for everyone to see, with two *R*s, an *E*, and a *Y* on the end.

The film was a Jim Carrey vehicle from start to finish. His manic moves and rubbery faces were scattered throughout. In fact, very little remained of the original script for the movie—even during filming, Carrey and *Ace Ventura*'s director, Tom Shadyac, constantly worked and reworked it to make the most of Carrey's unique brand of comedy.

But by February 1994, Carrey's work on the movie was long finished. It was up to the filmgoing public to give a "thumbs up" or "thumbs down" to the job he had done. Jim had poured his heart and soul into the project, and now it was the moment of truth. Carrey figured that the film would do one of two things: either launch his movie career or keep him out of motion pictures for years.

Jim Carrey had wanted very much for the character of Ace Ventura to be unlike anything viewers had ever seen. But had he gone too far? Would the American public laugh along with him? Or would they turn away in distaste?

As Carrey and Flemming looked for Jim's name up on the marquees of Atlanta, they also saw something on the sidewalks below that neither comedian had counted on: lines of people waiting to see Jim's movie. Long lines. In just that first weekend, *Ace Ventura* was well on its way to grossing a total of $12 million.

Because he had been accustomed to hearing the immediate response of a live audience during years of stand-up comedy, Carrey wanted to sneak into one of the theaters to watch the film along with an audience who was seeing it for the first time. He had almost pulled it off when that theater's manager recognized him and had his staff members

trail him into the theater. The house lights were still bright; the audience got a good look at Jim Carrey, while a group of theater employees repeatedly squawked "the eagle has landed" into their walkie-talkies. So much for anonymity.

On the Monday morning after the movie's premiere, Wayne Flemming heard about the incredible success of the film in its first weekend. The magnitude of what had happened in the previous three days registered right away. People all over America had flocked to see his friend's movie. A nation of moviegoers had plunked down their ticket money, cozied up to buckets of popcorn, and laughed their way through *Ace Ventura, Pet Detective*. All those dollars—and a little bit of common sense—told

Carrey as mad scientist Edward Nygma and Val Kilmer as millionaire Bruce Wayne in the 1994 movie Batman Forever.

Wayne that his old buddy was a now a big star. But when Wayne tried to convey that idea to his friend, a dazed Jim Carrey could only reply, "I don't believe it."

Before *Ace Ventura, Pet Detective* had even gone into production, a movie director named Charles Russell was making plans to create a second film starring Jim Carrey. *The Mask*, based on a Dark Horse Comic Book character, would be produced by New Line Cinema. Russell, who was responsible for pre-production on *The Mask*, had caught Carrey's stand-up act in 1986 and knew right away that he wanted Carrey for the title role. He instructed the film's screenwriter, Mike Werb, to be certain to customize the script to highlight Carrey's wide-ranging talents.

Werb was somewhat taken aback by the assignment since he had no idea who Jim Carrey was. He had never seen the TV series *In Living Color*, and *Ace Ventura* was not even in production yet. But Werb got plenty of input from Russell, who knew instinctively that Carrey's gift for impressions, his rubberized facial expressions and elastic body movements, and his willingness to sing and dance made him perfect for the part.

So, without ever having seen Carrey and before Carrey had even agreed to do the film, Werb undertook the task of writing a script for him. Carrey would eventually sign on to do the film, which went into production in the fall of 1993 and was released on July 29, 1994.

Ace Ventura's huge success landed Carrey a $7-million contract to make a third movie, called *Dumb and Dumber*. He was granted creative control over the project by New Line Cinema, and he was also allowed to choose his costar, Jeff Daniels. *Dumb and Dumber* went into production in the spring of 1994, on the heels of *The Mask*, and was released during the lucrative holiday season. It immediately became the top-grossing film of the season, primarily because it appealed to adolescents. It was Jim Carrey's third major motion picture in 12 months.

If Jim Carrey had had any doubts about his fame being

real, they were gone by this time. People, including his own relatives, were asking for his autograph. But his joy in finally having "made it" in the film business was tempered by his grief over the loss of his father, Percy Carrey, who had given his son guidance and inspiration.

Soon after losing his father, however, Carrey was fortunate to be able to distract himself from the sorrow he felt by focusing on his work. In the fall of 1994 he started on his next project, playing the Riddler in *Batman Forever*. Jim's role demanded his full attention, both physically and mentally, and took his mind off his father's death, at least temporarily. It helped, too, that Jim had the ear of a sympathetic Batman—actor Val Kilmer, who understood Jim's situation too well. Kilmer had lost his father a few years earlier, just before he started work on the movie *Tombstone*. Although the two actors battled on the big screen as Batman and the Riddler, they were anything but enemies offscreen. Carrey felt comfortable talking to Kilmer about his emotions because of their similar experiences.

Perhaps only another celebrity would truly be able to understand Carrey's situation. What happened at his father's funeral—his relatives had pestered him for his autograph—wouldn't happen to someone who isn't famous, or who hasn't earned some sort of notoriety or attracted admirers. Jim Carrey wasn't interested in a rating of his fame in September 1994 when he said a last good-bye to his father, but he got one nonetheless.

Among Jim Carrey's early—and unsuccessful—film roles was his portrayal of a high schooler named Mark Kendall in the 1985 movie Once Bitten.

2

CARREYS, CANUCKS, AND CAMPERS

PERCY CARREY WAS a jazzman. He played both the saxophone and the clarinet, and he even had his own orchestra in Toronto for a while. But when his wife, Kathleen, gave birth to their first child, Percy sold his saxophone.

The new father wasn't concerned that the spirited saxophone music would waken his newborn daughter, however. He was concerned that a musician couldn't support a family. Years later, during an interview with *Playboy* magazine, Jim Carrey likened the actions of his father, Percy, to a scene from a movie. "It was like a Hollywood script," said Jim. "He sold his sax to get my sister out of the hospital when she was born. And he never went back to music."

With his family in mind, Percy took on a more reliable job as an accountant. For 26 years he reported to work as a company controller as he watched his young family grow. Kathleen and Percy were blessed with another daughter and two sons. Their youngest child, James Eugene Carrey, was born on January 17, 1962, in Newmarket, Ontario.

Jim would later tell *People* magazine that his middle name must

The skyline of Toronto, Ontario, dominated by the CN Tower (center). Although the capital of Ontario is one of several large cities in Canada and one of the most cosmopolitan cities in North America, Canadian Jim Carrey learned that many Americans tend to view their northern neighbors as rural and unsophisticated.

have been his parents' way of keeping him humble. For sure enough, "Eugene" was soon shortened to "Gene," and "Jim" transformed to "Jimmy," and a young, skinny, Jim Carrey became saddled with the nickname "Jimmy Gene the String Bean." Not that he didn't earn the nickname— the tall, thin kid drove his parents to distraction by frequently refusing to eat.

The budding entertainer turned his family's dinner table into a stage for his earliest performances. With this captive crowd, the little boy who wouldn't eat entertained his family by making funny faces. According to Scott and Barbara Siegel, the authors of *The Jim Carrey Scrapbook*, the same "act" might also appear in the basement after dinner, especially when the Carreys had company. It didn't take much encouragement from his family to convince Jimmy Gene the String Bean to try out his assortment of impressions on guests. Television performers, members of the family, and nearby neighbors all found their way into Jimmy Gene's repertoire. Even at an early age, making people laugh made Jim Carrey happy.

Before he discovered his ability to entertain others, Jim reports, he was content to spend his time quietly drawing. But as he began to realize that making people laugh supplied a means to make friends, he took some of his impressions on the road—during school recesses. His playground performances were well received. In an interview with *Saturday Night Magazine*, he describes how his impressions caused his miraculous transformation into a popular kid: "That was when I broke out of my shell at school, because I really didn't have any friends or anything like that. . . . Finally I did this zany thing, and all of a sudden I had tons of friends."

And he owed it all to his ability to impersonate just about anyone, including the school principal.

When *Nickelodeon Magazine* asked Jim Carrey to name his first real stage performance, he had to confess to being somewhat of a class cutup as early as second grade. Even so, he was a very good student. "I was in music class and we were practicing for the Christmas assembly. One day I started fooling around by mocking the musicians on a record. The teacher thought she'd embarrass me by making me get up and do what I was doing in front of the whole class." That tactic might have worked on other students, but in Carrey's case, it failed to produce the embarrassment the music teacher had expected. Instead, Jim put on a stellar performance in front of the entire class. Even the teacher couldn't help laughing. She then rewrote the Christmas program to include Jim's routine. Jim was happy to comply with his teacher's request to perform before the entire assembly. "That," Jim told *Nickelodeon Magazine*, "was the beginning of the end."

Five grades later, another teacher would find herself

negotiating with Jim to keep order in her classroom. Jim has told several interviewers about the deal he struck with his seventh-grade teacher: the last 15 minutes of each class were allotted for Jim to perform a comedy routine—*if* he didn't fool around *during* the class. This agreement, hammered out without any agents or managers, worked wonderfully for Jim and his teacher. "I'd sit there and finish my work, then start working on my set," Carrey explained to the *Fort Worth Star-Telegram*.

The importance of that simple but effective truce wasn't lost on Carrey. Nor has he lost touch with his seventh-grade teacher. Jim told *Nickelodeon Magazine* that she recently sent him several of his early pieces of art—including "Teacher with an Ax Through Her Head"—that she had saved all these years. Perhaps she had some inkling then of the talent that her "star" pupil possessed.

Tales like this would later serve Carrey well in his comedy routines, as would his stories of growing up in Canada. He and his siblings grew up around Toronto, Ontario, in Aurora, Jackson's Point, and Burlington. Jim's Canadian childhood would serve him well in his comedy routines when he included his impression of how Americans tend to view their northern neighbors. Although Canada has several major, modern cities such as Toronto, many Americans still think of it as a vast rural region, filled with elk, bears, Canada geese, and miles of snowy country. So, despite the fact that Jim grew up near a busy city, he would one day showcase himself as the stereotypical backwoods "Canuck" (a term used to describe French Canadians), tromping through the forests and poking fun at the popular American misconception that all Canadians are unsophisticated woodsmen.

In his November 1991 comedy special, "Unnatural Act," Jim described his homeland by using every conceivable cliché about Canada. "Yes, Canada," he mused. "It was a frozen, hostile wasteland. And there was much work to be done if we were to survive the elements. After boring a hole through the ice to find food, my good friend Nanook and I would build an igloo to protect ourselves from polar bears . . . and flying hockey pucks."

That sketch and his nightclub routine were based not only on Canadian stereotypes but also on an activity that Jim's dad enjoyed. Each year around the winter holidays, Percy and his children would don stocking caps and arm themselves with axes. With these minimal props, they'd set off for the road in front of their home, where passing tourists could view the Carrey family interpretation of the "bringing home the tree" tradition.

The memory is obviously a merry one for Jim, who also remembers festive butter fights at the Carrey family dinner table, as he told Erik Hedegaard in the 1994 interview "Nobody's Fool" for *Details* magazine. During that interview and in others, Jim has proclaimed himself only the second-funniest member of his family. He lovingly bestows the honor of funniest upon his father.

In many interviews, including those with Barbara Walters and *Parade*, *Playboy*, and *People* magazines, Carrey describes his Canadian childhood as basically happy. He speaks of family togetherness and lots of love and laughter. As he told Barbara Walters, "I got a lot of support from my parents. That's the one thing I always appreciated. They didn't tell me I was being stupid, they told me I was being funny."

Jim was funny. His dad was funny. But what happened in 1975, when Jim was 13, wasn't the least bit funny. Percy Carrey lost his job.

At 51, after having been in his job as controller for 26 years, Jim's dad was suddenly jobless. Worse yet, he couldn't find another accountant position anywhere. Desperate for work, Percy Carrey swallowed his pride and accepted a janitor's job in a factory so that his family could move into the inexpensive housing provided by the company. The Titan Wheels tire-rim factory of Scarborough, Ontario, soon had five more Carreys in its employ: every member of the family helped out by cleaning rest rooms.

As one might suspect, the teenaged Jim Carrey was not happy about the situation in which he and his family found themselves. This was definitely not cool. He vividly described the details of his demanding schedule to Barbara Walters: "I spent eight hours after school scraping pubic hair off urinals," he told her. The round-the-clock school-to-work-to-school schedule was exhausting. Before long Jim had trouble keeping his eyes open during school hours. Finally, after he turned 16, the funny, straight-A student who loved to make his classmates and teachers laugh dropped out of school. He was bitter and angry with the world, and he claims that he had no friends and didn't want any. Carrey told Erik Hedegaard that he was an angry "ninth grade dropout who moved through the factory with a baseball bat in his cart, pounding holes in the walls."

While Jim was venting some of his anger on factory walls, his father was seething inside. As if losing his job and his house weren't bad enough, Percy Carrey also had to endure the insults of his father-in-law, who didn't think much of the way that Percy was providing for his daughter and grandchildren. This was a painful period for Percy Carrey and one that Jim would never forget. "My grandparents were alcoholics," Jim told *Parade*, "and my grandfather would get my dad in a corner every Christmas and tell him what a loser he was because he didn't have a job. My father would just sit there and turn purple with anger."

Because Percy was such a nice man, Jim explained, he would just endure the browbeating without saying a word. But Jim hated watching his father quietly seethe with anger, and he used his sense of humor to try to ease these painful situations. "[A]s soon as my grandparents would leave, I'd imitate them," he said. "My father would be so relieved, it was as if I pulled the pressure plug when I went into this routine."

Time and time again, Jim's ability to impersonate and find humor in the darkest moments of life helped him to

save the day, at least for himself and his father. It was an outlet of sorts for them both—a release valve that lessened some of the pressures of a difficult life.

Jim was less able to amuse his mother, however, no matter how hard he tried. As time went by, his impersonations and his attempts at humor could not overcome her pain, be it real or imagined. Jim has described his mother as a "professional sick person" who took lots of pain pills as a way of getting attention. He developed his own perspective on his mom's behavior by constantly reminding himself that "she's the daughter of alcoholics who'd leave her alone at Christmas time." Imagining his mother's situation helped him to understand why she behaved the way she did. But Jim never stopped trying to make his mother laugh, although she would sometimes scream out in pain and ask him to leave her sickroom. The same child who wouldn't eat but had made Kathleen Carrey laugh still wanted to entertain her as she languished in her bed. But now, Jimmy Gene the String Bean was old enough to appreciate the reasons for her pain.

The cramped factory housing of Scarborough, Ontario, shown here, was home to the Carrey family for several years before Percy Carrey decided to leave his job and the Carreys began living in a van.

Jim Carrey on the stand-up comedy circuit in the 1980s.

3

FROM IMPERSONATOR TO ORIGINATOR

JIM'S DAD WAS convinced that one's dreams don't die just because of financial setbacks. Percy Carrey believed in his son's talent and continued to encourage him to pursue an entertainment career. In 1977, Jim turned 15, and in the midst of the family's turmoil and troubles, Percy Carrey saw that his youngest child was given the chance to make his dreams come true. He arranged a trial performance for Jim at the Yuk Yuk Comedy Club in Toronto, helped his son write his material, and even drove him to the club on the night he was scheduled to perform.

It did not go well.

In an interview with *Playboy* magazine, Jim described his disastrous debut on the professional comedy circuit. On the advice of his mother, Jim appeared onstage sporting a yellow polyester suit that she had chosen. Kathleen Carrey swore that "all the young men were wearing them—she'd seen it on 'Donohue,'" Jim recalled. Maybe his mom *had* seen entertainers wearing pastel polyester suits on the popular, long-running American daytime talk show. Maybe she had even seen members of the studio audience wearing yellow polyester suits. But Jim found out all too soon that no one in the clubs of Toronto did. Except him. So, on the one occasion when he wanted desperately to fit in, he instead stood out like a sore thumb. Already feeling self-conscious appearing on a professional stage for the first time in his life, Jim wore a suit so conspicuous that it made him look as if he were wearing a costume. He was embarrassed and humiliated, but it was too late to do anything about it. He had no choice but to wear the yellow suit onstage.

Strike one.

Jim clutched the ventriloquist's dummy he'd brought with him and went into his routine. But this wasn't the crowd Jim was accustomed to entertaining at recess, the Carreys' dinner table, or the end of class during the time set aside by his teacher. These people were nightclub customers who had paid to be entertained. They didn't know Jim Carrey and Jim Carrey didn't know them. He didn't know what to say or do to make his audience laugh. His material and delivery, like his clothes, were all wrong. His impressions weren't impressing anyone. Jim was moving through his repertoire of characters, but the crowd wasn't responding. The Yuk Yuk Comedy Club's audience didn't laugh at a single joke.

Strike two.

As if his chances of becoming a hit weren't already slim, Carrey told Barbara Walters, "the owner of the club had this little thing that he liked to do where he would stand backstage with a microphone and [use] all kinds of fun [sound] effects and heckle new comedians." Carrey remembers hearing the hurtful comments of the nightclub owner coming through the Yuk Yuk Club's sound system. It must have been hard for him to remain onstage when he heard "Totally b-o-r-i-n-g. Totally boring," blaring in the background as the owner kept up a running commentary on his act. Jim was having enough trouble trying to interest the audience in his routine or get them to respond to

Jim's first acting role was as a young cartoonist named Skip Tarkenton in the short-lived TV show The Duck Factory *(1984).*

something—anything.

The situation got worse by the minute. Among the sounds the nightclub owner broadcast was a clip from the soundtrack of the popular rock musical *Jesus Christ, Superstar*. It didn't take long for the audience to join in the heckling as they heard "Crucify him, crucify him!" over and over again through the sound system. Then the manager himself called out, demanding that Carrey leave the stage. Jim hadn't even finished the routine he and his dad had prepared.

Strike three.

Jim Carrey had struck out, and it would be two years before he was willing to step into the batter's box again.

Carrey's breakthrough on the comedy circuit came in 1981, when he began making regular appearances at the Comedy Store in Los Angeles. There he joined the ranks of other up-and-coming comedians such as Robin Williams, shown here with his Mork and Mindy *costar Pam Dauber.*

The fact that Jim Carrey ever returned to stand-up comedy at all was a testament to the lessons that the young man had learned from his family's misfortunes. He had seen his father lose his job and be forced to go from an accountant's office strewn with ledgers, adding machines, and calculators to a janitor's closet filled with mops, brooms, and toilet bowl brushes. He had seen him trade in his suit and tie for a maintenance worker's jumpsuit. He had witnessed Percy Carrey's humiliation when Jim's own grandfather verbally abused Percy for his shortcomings. He had moved with his family from their comfortable home into unfamiliar and cramped factory housing. But throughout all these troubles, Jim Carrey's father had persevered. He had kept the family together.

But Percy Carrey knew something was wrong when his family's mood teetered on frustration and its mindset bordered on racism. When the members of his once-happy family began blaming other racial groups for taking their jobs, he knew that they were simply trying to understand their own miserable plight. The Carreys began blaming anyone and anything for causing their own misfortune. Describing that painful period, Carrey says, "the whole family was turning into monsters."

Percy Carrey didn't like what was happening to his family. Rather than see his loved ones become hateful and resentful, Percy decided that the Carreys had to quit their jobs at the tire-rim factory, even if it meant moving out of factory housing. Even if it meant that "home" for the Carrey clan would now be a Volkswagen camper.

When the Carreys moved into their VW van, they may have been sinking into poverty, but they were rising above ignorance and prejudice. They were also refusing to accept defeat. His father's decision proved to be another monumental lesson for the youngest Carrey. Jim summed it up for *Parade* magazine in this way: "Failure taught me that failure isn't the end unless you give up."

When it came to his dream of becoming a performer, Jim Carrey also wasn't giving up. Not the boy who had spent hours in his room making countless faces in the mirror. He had kept his family in stitches at the dinner table with his impersonations. He had mimicked the voices and facial expressions of others to win friends on the school playground. He had won 15 minutes of class time each day for his comedy routine.

When Barbara Walters asked Jim Carrey why he didn't just give up, he answered, "I couldn't. I mean, I don't have a trade." Maybe Jim didn't have a trade, but he did have a craft. He had been practicing that craft and perfecting his skills since he was a toddler. And all of the work was about to pay off.

Jim Carrey wasn't wearing a yellow polyester suit when he took to the stage in 1979, two years after his disastrous debut. The club owner didn't heckle him, and the nightclub audience didn't boo him offstage. They were all too busy laughing. And that is exactly what Jim wanted.

Inspired by comedian and impressionist Rich Little (shown here in 1983 imitating comedian Groucho Marx), Jim Carrey filled his early stand-up routines with impressions of famous personalities.

Before long, Carrey's offbeat humor and exaggerated facial expressions were winning him comedy gigs all over Canada. He was 17 years old, and his career as a stand-up comedian was now successfully underway. And since Percy Carrey couldn't always chauffeur his son to and from performances as he had done at the Yuk Yuk Comedy Club, the likable Jim managed to find a way home with other performers on the nightclub circuit. One night, stand-up comedian Wayne Flemming drove Jim back from a gig at a Toronto nightclub. As he followed Jim's directions, he wondered why he was being asked to pull up to a Volkswagen camper. He was surprised when

Carrey explained, "That is where we all sleep."

Funnyman Jim Carrey wasn't joking. That camper was still home for the Carreys. For a time, they even moved out of the camper and pitched a tent on a relative's lawn. But Canadian winters can be long and cold, and they couldn't stay there for long without freezing.

Fortunately, Jim wasn't the only member of his family to find work. Slowly but surely, after eight months of a vagabond life, all of the Carreys found work and were able to move back into a house.

Getting to know Jim Carrey at this time in his life might have been a little difficult. He was never himself. He was always impersonating someone. Onstage, he could imitate just about anyone. Audience members would call out names of famous people and Carrey would impersonate them on command, transforming himself into Mahatma Gandhi or Clint Eastwood or even Cher, right before their eyes and ears. His success on the Canadian comedy circuit earned him rave reviews—and the confidence he needed to try his act at the Comedy Store, the hottest comedy spot in Los Angeles, California.

The teenaged Carrey wasn't ready for Los Angeles, however. Nor was Los Angeles ready for Jim Carrey. Los Angeles is a big city, and its audiences thought Jim's act was "small town," not sophisticated enough for their tastes. Carrey soon went back to Canada, to the audiences who knew and loved him. But he had seen what to expect from Los Angeles, and he spent the next two years polishing and perfecting his act. By the time he headed to Los Angeles again at 19, Jim Carrey was ready.

He started out small. Using the list of phone contacts he'd put together in Canada, he found work doing comedy at some of the lesser-known clubs in Los Angeles, staying at a low-rent hotel along Sunset Strip and trying to stretch out the thousand dollars he had saved in Canada. He also made several appearances at a few small clubs in New York City. But in the early 1980s, any comedian who was worth his or her salt had to make it at L.A.'s Comedy Store, the same club where Jim had once bombed. Jim knew that he was no exception—he had to win over the Comedy Store crowd himself.

That he did. Before long, Jim Carrey was a regular at the famous club. His impressions were a hit, and even though he was only pulling down $25 a night, he was working with the likes of Robin Williams and Arsenio Hall. And as he fielded requests for impressions from the audience, he was also fielding some impressive offers to work on the nightclub stages of Las Vegas, Nevada.

One of the best offers came from veteran comedian Rodney Dangerfield, who caught Carrey's act at the Comedy Store and loved it. The comedian whose trademark line is "I don't get no respect" surely respected Jim Carrey's talent. Dangerfield had a nightclub act in Las Vegas and needed someone to "open" for him—to go onstage first and warm up the audience before he did his own act. Dangerfield wanted Jim Carrey.

After opening for Dangerfield, Carrey was soon sought after to open for other top-name entertainers. For the next several years, the kid from Canada not only opened for Dangerfield, but also for singers such as the Pointer Sisters, Andy Williams, Sheena Easton, and Pat Boone.

Jim Carrey's star appeared to be rising. Work was steady enough and the money was good enough that Jim could afford to move his parents from Toronto to Los Angeles. At the time, it seemed like the right thing to do.

Unfortunately, it wasn't such a good idea after all. The timing was terrible. For all his success, Jim Carrey wasn't happy with the work he was doing onstage. He was tired of imitating others, and he started turning down gigs that required him to do endless impersonations. His fellow comics thought he was a fool to refuse such offers, but Carrey was convinced that he had to stop imitating everybody else to succeed. To make matters worse, he felt obligated to support his parents. This was not a good time to be turning down work.

Carrey's parents began to count on him for their livelihood. "[They] were putting pressure on me to be the star, to save their lives and to buy them the big house with the pillars, like Elvis, you know?" said Jim. "And it came to a head. I had no money. I had no jobs. . . . They were really lovely people, but they got caught up in thinking that they were going to be taken care of."

Jim began having trouble sleeping; he had nightmares and anxiety attacks, and he feared he was having a nervous breakdown. He has told numerous interviewers that he resented the pressure he felt from his parents, but he knew that there was more to his difficulties than that. He wanted to be himself, both onstage and at home, and he didn't feel he was being allowed that chance.

Finally, in 1984, Jim signed on as the lead in a television series called *The Duck Factory*. He wouldn't be doing impersonations in this role. Instead, he'd be acting, playing the role of a young cartoon artist named Skip Tarkenton. Jim's character was a naive newcomer to Los Angeles, an innocent kid from the Midwest who finds himself surrounded by street-smart city slickers.

Unfortunately, Skip Tarkenton's character had been developed before Jim was signed to do the role, so the part was not at all tailored to showcase Jim's comedic talents. In fact, Skip defined normalcy on the show while all the other characters were offbeat. NBC gave the show a fighting chance by scheduling it directly after the popular *Cosby Show*, but even so the series folded after just 13 weeks. And when the show ended, Carrey's financial stability ended too.

It wasn't easy for any of the Carreys, but Jim knew what he had to do. He packed up his parents and moved them back to Toronto. He continued to love and support them, both emotionally and financially, but now he did so from a more comfortable distance. He began taking acting lessons. He wrote poetry, sculpted, and painted. And he continued to open for Rodney Dangerfield in Vegas—but not as an impressionist. This time, the comic wasn't imitating anyone; he was doing original material that showcased his own talents. Jim Carrey was coming into his own at last.

In March 1987 Jim married an actress whom he'd met some years earlier at Mitzi Shore's Comedy Store. Melissa Womer had been a waitress there when Jim was plying his comedy act. They dated for several years before marrying. Soon after, while Jim was in the midst of revamping his stage act and comedy routines, he and Melissa added to their resumés the new roles of Mom and Dad. They became the parents of a baby girl in September of that year. To Jim, all of his accomplishments—past, present, and future—suddenly paled compared to being Dad to daughter Jane.

It was even more important now for Carrey to keep his opening gig with Rodney Dangerfield. The older comedian got into the habit of watching Jim Carrey's performances from the wings before taking the stage himself. Shielded from the audience by the curtains fringing the stage, Dangerfield could watch both Carrey and the audience without being seen himself.

On some nights, Dangerfield marveled at the young comedian's courage in trying out new material. He knew how difficult it was to play to a crowd that wasn't laughing. For if anyone knows what it is like to go onstage and bomb, it is another entertainer who has had to endure the same painful experience.

It would have been very easy for Jim Carrey to abandon his new routines and revert to doing impressions, which had made people laugh and made money for him. In fact, had Carrey been opening for any other entertainer, he might have been asked to continue using the material that had gotten him this far. Fortunately for Carrey, Dangerfield understood the transition he was trying to make and believed in Carrey's talent. So the veteran comedian let the

young comic feel his way through—testing new material, audiences' reactions, and himself.

Sometimes the audience didn't get Jim's material at all. Some nights he would take the stage without any idea of where his routine would end up. He had no scripted monologue, no prepared jokes, and no well-rehearsed impressions. During this transitional period, which began in 1985 and lasted through 1988, Jim Carrey just headed out into the spotlight every evening with spiked hair and big red pants. What would happen onstage on any given night was anyone's guess. By his own admission, his act was "total improvisation." Carrey might begin by talking about one subject, then suddenly start writhing around on the stage as "Snake Boy."

Sometimes, when nothing he did or said was getting a laugh, Jim would simply sink to the floor of the stage and

Carrey attributes much of his stand-up success to veteran comedian Rodney Dangerfield, shown here during a nightclub act. "[I]f I was making him laugh," Carrey said of Dangerfield, "I knew I was on to something."

sit there, pretending to be chatting with his wife. He would tell her how they "would soon be living on Easy Street" before breaking into tears. It was a dark, different type of comedy.

Jim remembers, "Many, many nights, I got no reaction at all. Rodney would watch me from the wings, standing there in his housecoat, and I'd come off stage and he'd shake his head and say, 'Those people were looking at you like you were from another planet.'"

Fortunately, there were also nights when Jim's new material "reached" the crowd and made them laugh. Eventually, Carrey discovered the right mix of imitation and originality that gained approval from audiences and made all of his struggling and testing worthwhile. But first Carrey had to convince those in charge on the comedy circuit that he was capable of doing more than imitating others. Although Carrey has never totally abandoned his impersonations, they eventually became just "dressing" to enhance his other material.

During this period, some club owners weren't comfortable with Jim's new style and still demanded that he perform only his tried-and-true impressions. But Jim held fast to his convictions and wouldn't back down. He let the club owners know, in no uncertain terms, that from that time on Jim Carrey would only perform his new material. Carrey now gave club owners two options—either let him perform his new kind of comedy in their clubs or fire him.

Those who chose to hire Jim Carrey during this stage in his life had the chance to see his unique brand of comedy emerge from the safety net of his old impressions. He was creating a stage persona for himself that would never again be confused with that of another performer.

To this day, Carrey credits Rodney Dangerfield with having helped "a young impressionist from Canada who dreamed, at one time, of being the next Rich Little." (At the time, Rich Little was the premier impressionist of the entertainment industry.) When Dangerfield first "hired me to open for him at Caesar's Palace in Las Vegas, it was a very big deal for me," Carrey admits. But in the end, what may have been even more important to the struggling young comedian was the sound of Rodney Dangerfield laughing in the wings. Maybe the audience didn't always get his humor, says Jim, "but if I was making [Dangerfield] laugh, I knew I was on to something." It was a vote of confidence Carrey sorely needed.

Jim Carrey won't soon forget hearing that sound. He has great respect for the comedian who jokingly claims that he gets none. Rodney Dangerfield not only gave Carrey a big break by asking him to be his opening act but also served as an important reminder that success doesn't always come overnight. In all, Carrey spent 15 years doing stand-up comedy and trying to make a name for himself, and through it all he always thought of Dangerfield's experience. "Sometimes," Carrey said, "the only thing that kept me going was the thought that Rodney made it when he was in his 50's."

In February 1995, at the American Comedy Awards, Jim got a chance to thank Rodney Dangerfield publicly for his help and inspiration. Carrey was thrilled to have been chosen to present Dangerfield with the Award for Creative Achievement. Standing at the podium in a crowded auditorium and in front of a huge television audience, Carrey described how instrumental the elder comedian had been in helping him get started in show business. He thanked Dangerfield for helping him to stay motivated during all those years on the comedy circuit. "In a business that generally values youth before talent," said Carrey, "he was absolute proof that it's never too late to make your mark. You may have to quit for a while and sell some paint, but you don't have to give up your dreams. So, on behalf of all the fans and performers that he inspired and helped along the way, I am deeply honored to present Rodney Dangerfield [with] this year's American Comedy Award for Creative Achievement."

The 1990 cast of In Living Color, *clockwise from top left: Jim Carrey, Tommy Davidson, Kelly Coffield, Damon Wayans, David Alan Grier, Kim Wayans, T'Keyah Crystal Keymah, Keenen Ivory Wayans, and Kim Coles.*

4

MANTRAS ON MULHOLLAND

FOR YEARS, JIM CARREY seemed to get by almost entirely on hopes and dreams. They fueled his imagination and kept him going when paychecks were scarce.

Of course, Carrey was actively looking for work as well. In the late 1980s, he even auditioned for the popular and prestigious late-night TV series *Saturday Night Live* (or *SNL*). Since think-on-your-feet improvisation was Jim's forte, joining an ensemble cast that performed live each week seemed to be the perfect move. It would help him gain widespread recognition by giving him weekly exposure on national television. Alas, Jim didn't stand a chance of making the show. His audition was affected by an incident that was completely out of his control.

When he arrived at the Burbank, California, studios of NBC, a terrible scene was unfolding:

I got out of my car, started walking through the parking lot, and I heard "Don't jump! Don't jump!" I looked up to the top of the roof, and there was a guy in a blue blazer trying to work up his nerve to throw himself

off the building. The whole time I was in there audition-
ing, I was thinking, "Is he dead? Is he dead yet?"

Thankfully, the man in the blue blazer didn't jump from
the building's rooftop after all. But the goings-on outside
the studio affected Jim's performance. *SNL* was not
thrilled at the chance to have Carrey join the cast. He
didn't get the job. (Ironically, Jim was a celebrity guest
host for *SNL* many years later, on May 18, 1996. Having
"made it" as a comedian, he opened for a show whose
directors hadn't thought he was good enough to be a
member of the regular cast.)

With no steady work and only sporadic gigs, Carrey
had a lot of time to think about his life and career, about
where he'd been so far and where he was headed. His
childhood dreams of becoming famous had taken him to
Toronto and on to "Tinseltown," as Hollywood, California, is often known, but still wasn't exactly sure why. He
needed to find out.

Carrey remembered that when he was a kid growing up
in Canada he had idolized the American movie actor
Jimmy Stewart. He had watched Stewart's movie *Mr.
Smith Goes to Washington* each time it was rerun on television. When video rental stores sprang up, Jim rented and
watched the film over and over. He remembers falling
asleep cradling the videocassette to his chest, praying that
some day he would follow in Stewart's footsteps. Perhaps
without realizing it then, Carrey was imagining what he
wanted to do when he grew up. The boy may have drifted
off to sleep, but the seed had been planted in his mind: he
wanted to be a movie star.

So, after Jim Carrey had become an entertainer and
established stand-up comedian and began to feel that he
had reached a crossroads in his career, he started thinking
about his childhood screen idol. No longer just a Canadian kid, Carrey was now in Hollywood, the movie capital
of the world. Maybe this was the next step—to make
movies. He was definitely in the right place. All he had to

do was talk himself into trying it. And that is exactly what he did.

Jim drove up Mulholland Drive to a vantage point high on a hill. From his car, he could see Hollywood sprawled before him. More important, in his mind's eye he could see his future in film. He explains:

> I've always believed in magic. When I wasn't doing anything in this town, I'd go up every night, sit on Mulholland Drive, look out at the city, stretch out my arms and say, "Everybody wants to work with me. I'm a really good actor. I have all kinds of great movie offers." I'd just repeat these things over and over, literally convincing myself that I had a couple of movies lined up. I'd drive down that hill, ready to take the world on, going, "Movie offers are out there for me, I just don't hear them yet." It was like total

Among Jim Carrey's film idols was actor Jimmy Stewart, shown here with Jean Arthur and Thomas Mitchell in the 1939 movie Mr. Smith Goes to Washington.

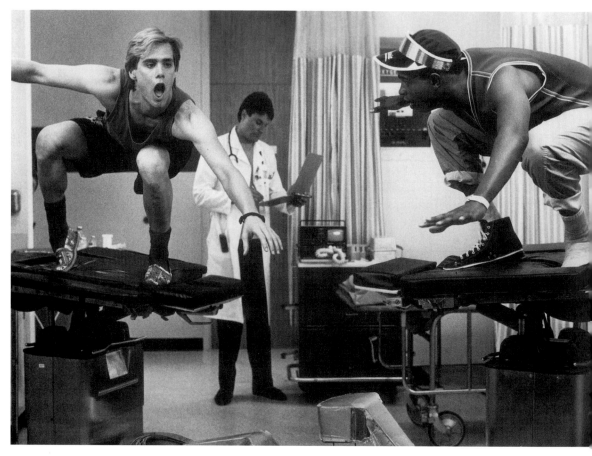

Carrey (left) and Damon Wayans are aliens who are transformed into California surfers in the 1989 movie Earth Girls Are Easy.

affirmations, antidotes to the stuff that stems from my family background, from knowing how things can go sour.

Jim hadn't forgotten the problems he and his family had faced. He was reminded of them every time he saw homeless people trying to eke out an existence on the streets. He tried not to dwell on the hard times he'd been through; instead, he imagined good times ahead. Still, at times sad thoughts got the better of him, and he would struggle with the nightmarish images that filled his head.

In time, however, Carrey learned to vent his anger and to clear his head of unpleasant thoughts. He even found a way to release his pent-up frustrations by channeling some of his troublesome thoughts into material for his comedy sketches. Jim admits that he sometimes looked out at an audience and felt just a bit smug. After all, he thought, there he was onstage letting off steam and speaking his mind while the poor audience members had no release valves of their own. Carrey believes that one of the advantages of being in the comedy business is that he can let all of his emotions out in this way. "I have to have an outlet," he readily admits, "or I'll explode."

With this newly discovered way of eliminating bad thoughts, Jim Carrey set about doing some positive thinking. He found himself driving up Mulholland Drive time and time again, telling himself he was a really good actor, and reminding himself that movie offers were out there for him. Perhaps it worked; in 1989, Jim landed the role of an alien in the movie *Earth Girls are Easy*. In the film, he and his fellow aliens, played by actors Jeff Goldblum and Damon Wayans, wind up slightly off-course and crash-land on the planet Earth—more specifically, in the Los Angeles backyard swimming pool of an earthling manicurist played by Geena Davis.

At last, Carrey was on his way to a career in film. The "mantra" he had used on Mulholland Drive had worked— there were movie offers out there for him. He has summed up his good fortune in this way:

> See, I've always believed that everything I've wanted, prayed for, will come to me in one way or another. I'm really careful about what I ask for. I asked God when I was young to give me whatever I need to help me be a great actor-comedian.

In *Earth Girls*, Carrey plays a big red alien named Wiploc who, with his fellow space travelers, undergoes a radical transformation at the Curl Up and Dye beauty salon and looks for all the world like another tall, blond surfer. But he nearly blows his cover when he gets behind the wheel of an automobile because his driving techniques are out of this world. Wiploc has to stick his head out of the driver's window of the beach-bound station wagon to see the highway: unfamiliar with cars, he steers with his feet. For the first time, moviegoers see what has since become Jim Carrey's trademark driving style.

Carrey made a valuable acquaintance with his *Earth Girls* costar Damon Wayans, who introduced him to his older brother Keenen Ivory. Keenen was in the process of casting for his new comedy-variety television show for the Fox network, and Carrey auditioned for the series. This time, there were no dire situations outside the studio, and Jim's audition went smoothly. In 1990, Carrey signed on as a cast member of the weekly show *In Living Color*.

Unlike his earlier television experience as a ready-made character on *The Duck Factory*, this time Jim was allowed to contribute to his character's development. In fact, he was given free rein to create numerous characters for the program's skits and sketches. *In Living Color* regularly brought Jim Carrey into the living rooms of America, and as he displayed his talent for zany impressions, his fan club grew. Soon, viewers were tuning in just to catch his creations.

One of Carrey's characters, a lame-brained public servant named Fire Marshall Bill, caused quite a stir. Reportedly, a national coalition of fire prevention groups asked that sketches involving the character be pulled off the air. They believed that Fire Marshall Bill set a bad example for children because he did not accurately represent firefighters. On the other hand, many police officers who watched the show really liked the character—for once, they said, someone was not poking fun at *them*. In addition to protest mail from firefighters, Carrey also received lots of fan mail from police officers who might have heard one too many cops-love-doughnuts jokes.

The next four years proved very educational for Jim Carrey. He learned his trade by becoming more adept at writing skits and creating characters as he helped to churn out the weekly show. The hectic schedule made him all the more aware of television's fast pace, which rarely allows writers or entertainers the luxury of revisions and retakes. During his stint on television, Carrey realized that some things happen only in the movies. But it wasn't necessarily a sad revelation for him—the movie offers he had assured himself were out there as he sat on Mulholland Drive soon began to pour in.

Carrey displays Ace's trademark hair and creative clothing style in Ace Ventura, Pet Detective.

5

AN *ACE* UP
HIS SLEEVE

IT DIDN'T MATTER that most of the comedians in Hollywood had already seen the script and had turned it down. Nor did it matter that Jim Carrey himself hated the original script and had resisted the project for two years. In the end, Carrey accepted the starring role in *Ace Ventura, Pet Detective*—and the rest, as they say, is history. After three years of churning out weekly TV episodes of *In Living Color*, Jim wanted a vehicle that he could fine-tune, one that gave him time to tinker with every action and reaction in a script before the final product went before an audience. Having been given free rein to tailor the movie's script to his own style, Carrey viewed *Ace Ventura* as the perfect opportunity to do so.

Throughout the film's shooting in Miami, Florida, Jim Carrey and director Tom Shadyac worked and reworked the script. Morgan Creek, the producer of *Ace Ventura*, had given Carrey creative control of the project, allowing him to make wholesale changes in the original script. He and Shadyac made full use of this opportunity to tailor the title role to Jim's talents.

Jim had definite ideas about who he wanted Ace to be. Confident to the point of being cocky, Ace always knows just what he wants to say and do, without a moment's hesitation. He never second-guesses himself because he is always right the first time. Carrey also wanted Ace to be extremely intelligent, with the instincts of a super-sleuth like the fictional Sherlock Holmes. Carrey wanted him to have a way with women but trouble with authority. And he wanted Ace to stand out in a crowd, to have a "look" that's all his own.

Without a doubt, Ace Ventura's appearance is unique. Not many Floridians opt to wear buckled leather boots in the sweltering heat of the South, but Ace does. Tucked into the boots are a pair of skin-tight striped pants. (Ace seems to own many similar pairs.) Tucked into his pants is a plain white T-shirt, worn under one of a number of Hawaiian-print shirts, each of which clashes horribly with any and all of the pairs of striped pants. Ace's mom apparently never succeeded in convincing her child that stripes and prints don't match. Each day, Ace wears a variation of this self-designed uniform.

As if Ace's outfits aren't enough to attract attention, the film's hairdressers must have had a field day styling Jim's dark tresses for the film. No one alive has ever had hair like Ace's. Only the make-believe mascot of the Bob's Big Boy restaurant chain even comes close. Ace's hair defies gravity, rising to ridiculous heights on the top of his head and swooping to an incredibly thick ducktail at the nape of his neck. As Ace Ventura, Jim doesn't even have to open his mouth to get a laugh. The hair gets laughs on its own. Audiences can't help themselves.

But viewers don't get a glimpse of Ace's hair right away. In the movie's opening scene, detective Ace is disguised as a uniformed delivery man whose hair is hidden under his cap. Everyone who has ever received a package with damaged or broken contents has probably imagined the primitive delivery techniques employed by Ace. He

repeatedly drops his package, treating it as though it's a soccer ball in play before drop-kicking it down the length of an apartment building's hallway. Satisfied that the parcel's jingling contents are destroyed, he picks up the mangled package and knocks on the door of an apartment. He then involves the occupant in the long, drawn-out process of reporting the damage. It's all part of an elaborate ruse to allow Ace an opportunity to retrieve a stolen dog from the apartment. Bending down over the "petnapped" pooch, Ace replaces the real dog with a stuffed animal—and a copy of his own oversized business card—before he hightails it out of the building and down the street.

Thus audiences are introduced to the world's best—and only—pet detective, Ace Ventura. Viewers not yet convinced that Ace is a likable sort usually melt when Ace offers dinner to the newly rescued dog by pulling out a custom-made doggie dish from the ashtray of his car.

Director Tom Shadyac gives instructions through a bullhorn on the set of a movie shoot. Jim Carrey enjoyed filming Ace Ventura, Pet Detective *because Shadyac and Morgan Creek, the producer, allowed their star to define Ace's character as the filming progressed. Shadyac would later direct* Liar, Liar.

Those still reserving judgement are won over when Ace enters his apartment after a crazy car chase and an encounter with his landlord, who reminds him that pets are not allowed in the building. For as soon as the door closes behind the doggy detective, the pets he swore he did not have appear from every corner of the apartment, including the freezer and toilet. The film has just begun, but Ace Ventura, Pet Detective has already captured the hearts of his audience.

The film's small details and strategic one-liners have become comic standards. Within a week of *Ace Ventura*'s premiere, enchanted viewers were doing their own renditions of Ace's trademark lines, such as his patented "Reeeeally" and his hearty "Alllllllllrighty, then!"

Carrey claims to have developed the movie character from his revamped nightclub act. Describing Ace Ventura as his "stage persona," Carrey has told interviewers that he set out to assure his audiences that nothing bothered him and that they, too, had nothing to worry about during his performance. Comedy is not brain surgery, after all; it's entertainment, and it's fun. No subject is sacred; Carrey pokes fun at everyone and everything. He mimics accents, he does impressions, and he takes every scene to ludicrous lengths.

In Carrey's personal life, however, things weren't so funny. His marriage to Melissa Womer was failing; it ended in divorce soon after *Ace Ventura* became a hit. Carrey's critics were quick to find him guilty of needing people around him when things weren't going well but of striking out on his own when he's enjoying success.

While the tabloids speculated about the reasons for Carrey's failed marriage, Jim quietly assessed the situation himself. It wasn't hard for him to understand why his marriage to Melissa had been unsuccessful, especially now that he was finally doing what he wanted to do. He could see that his love for his work was so encompassing that it left little time for anything or anyone else. He was happy spending every waking moment thinking of ways to improve his latest project. But this attitude does not make for an attentive husband.

Jim Carrey readily admits that he isn't easy to live with. He sees how his devotion to his work would make almost any woman feel neglected. He laments that he may never be able to settle down happily with someone. For Carrey, trying to do so is perhaps one of the greatest challenges in his life.

Carrey as the "wound-up ball of spontaneous combustion" known as the Mask.

6

DANCING FOR DAD

AS JIM CARREY eventually found out, he was not alone in envisioning himself on the silver screen. Film director Charles Russell was also "seeing" Carrey in his upcoming movie. So clear was Russell's vision of what Carrey could bring to the screen that he had screenwriter Mike Werb tailor the title role in *The Mask* to Carrey's wide-ranging talents before Carrey had even signed on. Russell had witnessed the comedian's stream-of-consciousness nightclub act and knew that Carrey could take on *The Mask*'s demanding dual role as no one else could.

Russell then set about bringing this vision to film. He called on Carrey with a copy of the comic book upon which the film is based and described how he wanted to bring the cartoon character to life using a combination of Jim's impersonations and an arsenal of special effects. Russell's genuine enthusiasm easily convinced Carrey to accept the assignment. It would prove to be a wise decision.

The Mask began production in the fall of 1993, hot on the heels of *Ace Ventura, Pet Detective*, which was due to be released over the upcoming Christmas season. Jim was on a roll. Without catching his breath, he shifted gears, changed costumes, and threw himself into this next project.

Carrey was well-suited for playing both the banker Stanley Ipkiss and his alter ego, the Mask. Naturally, the character of Ipkiss seems mild compared to the larger-than-life Mask, but the quiet banker holds a special place in the heart of the actor who brought him to life on the screen. Carrey sees good-natured Stanley as the true hero of the film, and he modeled his portrayal of the character on a special hero from his own life. According to Jim, his father, Percy Carrey, provided much of the inspiration for Stanley. Carrey enjoyed playing Stanley Ipkiss so much that he once commented that he would have been comfortable playing only that role through the entire film.

In a word, Stanley Ipkiss is vulnerable. His innate goodness allows others to take advantage of him, and his acts of kindness never win the girl or get the promotion. On the road of life, he is standing on the curb, perfectly positioned to be splashed by passing cars. (In fact, that exact scenario takes place in the film.) For example, Stanley manages to finagle hard-to-get show tickets to impress a girl. She takes the tickets—and takes a girlfriend to the show. He receives only a thank-you for his efforts. And when he takes his car to an auto repair shop for a simple oil change, the unscrupulous mechanics not only rack up an astronomical repair bill, but they also leave him temporarily without his car, giving him no choice but to drive their nightmarish loaner car. The noxious heap of metal barely moves, and it embarrasses him in front of Tina, the very woman he has been trying to impress. Humiliated, he heads home with the car sputtering, smoking, hesitating, and lurching until it finally conks out on a bridge.

Despite his own troubles, when Stanley believes he sees a drowning man struggling in the river below, he feels compelled to do the right thing by jumping from the bridge, hollering that he knows CPR. For his admirable efforts, he finds only a floating tangled clump of seaweed

and debris, and he ruins his suit in the process. Amid the waterlogged waste, however, he finds a wooden mask, which intrigues him enough that he frees it from the tangled mess and takes it home.

He can't even get in the door of his apartment without a run-in with his landlady, who is maddeningly impossible to please. She berates and belittles the dripping, disheveled Stanley for ruining her new hallway floor. He cloisters himself in his apartment, contented that at least his dog, Milo, shows him affection, and he rewards himself for having survived a rough day by tuning out his life and turning on his favorite cartoons. Almost immediately he is

Stanley Ipkiss (Jim Carrey) attempts to find the answer to the wooden mask's mysterious powers by consulting Dr. Neuman (Ben Stein) in the 1993 movie The Mask. *Jim fashioned Ipkiss's character after his father, Percy Carrey.*

Charles Russell, director of The Mask*, was so certain of Jim Carrey's ability to bring the title character to life that he tailored the script to fit Carrey's talents before Carrey even agreed to do the film.*

loudly chastised for the noise by his landlady and switches off the TV, forgoing the only pleasure he has left.

Then he remembers the mask and feels strangely compelled to try it on. Instantly the meek, mild-mannered Stanley becomes a whirling dervish of energy as he is transformed into his alter ego, the Mask. In a conversation with reporters, actor Carrey calls the Mask a "wound-up ball of spontaneous combustion."

On screen the transformation is instantaneous, but for Carrey the process took four hours in the makeup chair. Every day. Apparently Kermit the Frog wasn't kidding when he moaned, "It's not easy being green." Carrey remembers that the long and involved daily makeup sessions just about drove him insane—which may or may not have prompted his *Mask* co-star, Cameron Diaz, to comment that working with Jim was not unlike visiting an insane asylum. To cope with the process, Jim would shut his mind off, letting it wander at will. After all, what else could he do?

The makeup sessions may have been trying, but the results were astounding. The Mask appears to have sprung right from the pages of a comic book—a life-sized, walking, talking comic-book character come to life. Both his head and his teeth are absurdly oversized, while his hair and his ears seem to be nonexistent. His massive green skull tapers to a narrow, cleft chin that accentuates every expressive movement of his mouth and those monstrously huge "pearly-whites."

The makeover was so impressive that Jim felt he had virtually become a cartoon character. Once the teeth were in place, he knew he had survived another makeup session and was ready for the cameras to roll. Even though Carrey played two roles in the film, which he admits made him feel somewhat schizophrenic, he never had any doubt about which character he was portraying at any given time—the makeup made the man. Stanley was meek and mild-mannered; the Mask was just the opposite.

And yet there is no real malice in the Mask character, as long as Stanley Ipkiss remains beneath the actual wooden mask. The viewer eventually learns that who is wearing the mask makes a big difference. When Stanley wears it, he overcomes his lack of social skills by becoming a terrific singer and dancer who attracts the woman of his dreams. Aside from the fact that the Mask does rob a bank to come up with a little spending cash—which he does without harming anyone—the Mask is not an evil character when Stanley wears the wooden mask.

But when the mask falls into the hands—or paws—of the movie's villain and of Milo the dog, the results are much different. It becomes truly menacing when it is put on by Dorian (played by Peter Greene), the force of evil in the movie. When Dorian is the Mask, it is purely evil, as is the man behind it. And when the scene-stealing mutt Milo puts on the mask, the results are hilarious. The smart, loyal little dog suddenly becomes a ferociously fanged canine out to exact revenge on anyone who has dared to mistreat his beloved owner. The filmmakers obviously had fun imagining what a puny pooch would do when given the chance to turn the tables on humans, and they brought their thoughts to the screen with an ample measure of humor.

Perhaps Jim Carrey himself best described the phenomenon of the mask when he talked about his enjoyment in playing the role of good guy Stanley Ipkiss. He said that Stanley had the spirit of the Mask inside him all along, even before he came across the actual mask floating in the river.

Charles Russell had made the right decision in casting Carrey for the title role in this movie. The filmmaker provided Carrey with the perfect stage for his repertoire of character impersonations by inserting scenes in which Carrey, as the totally uninhibited Mask, could change characters and costumes seemingly in mid-sentence. In one nightclub scene, for example, the Mask appears to be dying after having been shot repeatedly. In a wonderful satire of the long, drawn-out death scenes common in American western movies, the Mask sports a black cowboy hat, the requisite red bandanna, a snazzy Western-style shirt complete with snaps and decorative stitching, and a pair of six-shooters in black holsters.

Carrey milks the scene for all it's worth. Clutching his side, he delivers the last words of a dying cowboy, calling upon a cast of fictional and historical characters to provide him with the inspiration and voices for the soliloquy. He seamlessly invokes memories of everyone from Tiny Tim in Charles Dickens's novel *A Christmas Carol* to Clark Gable's Rhett Butler in the film *Gone With the Wind*. The show-within-a-show idea is not only funny, but it also underscores Carrey's wonderful gift for mimicry. The off-the-wall impressions are carefully linked to the movie's plot line, however—even the "bad guys" dab at tears as they, too, are taken in by the poignant last words of the Mask and Carrey's endless cast of characters. Finally the scene ends as abruptly as it began, as the Mask bounces away, unscathed by the bullets and ready to battle wits with the bad guys once again.

Carrey's expertise in doing impressions is understandable. He spent years honing his craft in nightclubs all over Canada and the United States. But what earned Jim even more kudos for his performance in *The Mask* was his newly acquired skill in singing and dancing. As he dips and twirls, lifts and spins his costar Cameron Diaz on the dance floor, he evokes the memory of one of the most famous film dancers, Fred Astaire.

The film's special effects make Carrey's dancing appear effortless, even as he lifts and catches his partner. But seeing Carrey bending impossibly at the waist to clench a rose in his teeth and remove it from a vase without using his hands makes it even more apparent why Russell wanted Carrey for this film. The director believes that Carrey's extreme flexibility and elasticized face saved thousands of dollars that he might have spent on special effects had he given the part to another actor. A viewer cannot always tell the difference between a movement made by Carrey himself and one created by special effects. Carrey is that good.

The actor also seemed completely at ease performing an elaborately staged song-and-dance number with dozens of uniformed police characters. As Cuban Pete, the Mask dons a black fringed sombrero and brandishes a pair of maracas, wowing the men and women of the police force sent to capture him. Only a few measures into the number, the police officers feel compelled to move to the Latin beat. They begin by rhythmically moving a shoulder here and there. Eventually, the entire force winds up surrendering themselves to a cop conga line, led by Cuban Pete.

By throwing himself into the song with such wild abandon, Carrey created one of the more memorable dance numbers in recent film history. As Lieutenant Mitch Kellaway, the detective in charge of the case, Peter Riegert adds a nice touch. Kellaway becomes disheartened at the sight of his hardened police force dancing the conga with the green-headed bank robber and threatens his partner, who shows signs of joining the dancers: "You start dancing, I'll blow your brains out." He is even more disconcerted when he learns that his conga-dancing force has made the 11 o'clock news.

Lieutenant Kellaway is one of several supporting characters who are fleshed out just enough to make the film work. Carrey's two characters would not work nearly as well if they were not constantly challenged by Greene's menacing Dorian or helped by Richard Jeni's banker, Charlie Schumaker, or Cameron Diaz's sympathetic Tina. Other minor characters, such as the irritating landlady and the crooked auto mechanics, are presented early on so that Stanley can later return as the Mask to seek revenge on them.

Audiences came away from *The Mask* marveling at

Cuban Pete compels the police officers sent to arrest him to join in a conga line in The Mask. *For this scene Carrey himself recorded the song "Cuban Pete," first made popular in the 1940s by musician and actor Desi Arnaz.*

Carrey's many talents. It was a smart move for him, but he was about to prove just how "stupid" he could be—for a fee of $7 million—when he launched himself into yet another project, a film called *Dumb and Dumber*, which began production in the spring of 1994.

It is unclear who gets top billing in the title of this film. It's a toss-up as to which character is less intelligent—Jim Carrey's Lloyd Christmas or Jeff Daniels's Harry Dunn. Both actors certainly throw themselves into their roles with gusto. Carrey uncapped a chipped tooth and allowed the film's hairdressers to give him a decidedly stupid-looking bowl cut. Daniels let his own hair grow long and then let the hairdressers style it into an idiotic, unkempt hairdo. Both men adopted goofy grins and loony laughs and perfected glassy-eyed stares to make themselves seem even more stupid.

Actress Lauren Holly plays the love interest for both men in *Dumb and Dumber*. Holly had turned down a part in *Ace Ventura, Pet Detective* (the part went to Courtney Cox, who went on to play Monica in the popular television show *Friends*). Holly's character, Mary, is idolized first by Lloyd and then by Harry.

Off-screen, Carrey's relationship with Holly was also warming up. The Hollywood version of their romance has them falling in love over a snowball fight on the set of *Dumb and Dumber*. Lauren Holly would become Jim Carrey's second wife in 1996, less than two years later. Carrey has told reporters that he is well aware of how corny it is to fall in love with a costar. But he also points out that when you do nothing but work on one movie after another, the only people you come in contact with are actors and film hands.

Jim was also happy to be working with actor Jeff Daniels. He admired the actor and hoped to learn more about acting from him. Carrey lobbied for Daniels to get the part of Harry Dunn. Having just finished *The Mask* for New Line Cinema, which would also produce *Dumb and Dumber*, Carrey now had some clout with the studio. So Jeff Daniels was hired even though the studio had never considered a serious actor such as Daniels.

Carrey was not only happy to work with Daniels, but also glad to have a costar who could shoulder some of the burden of carrying the film. Both *Ace Ventura* and *The Mask* were essentially one-man shows, which meant that Carrey's acting had to carry both films. He was the one who had to be funny, and he had to appear in nearly every scene in both films. On *Dumb and Dumber*, however, he felt that his workload was halved by Jeff Daniels. With Jeff as a costar, Carrey didn't even have to be in every scene. Since this was Carrey's third project in one year, he greatly appreciated the lighter load.

In *Dumb and Dumber*, Christmas and Dunn are a pair of down-and-out losers who not only are incredibly dumb, but who also seem to have extremely bad luck. Just when it appears that a situation can't possibly get worse, a bit of bad luck or a stupid move by either character proves that it can. Neither Lloyd nor Harry can keep a job, and what little money they do have is about to run out. Then Lloyd comes up with the crazy idea of traveling across the country to catch up with a pretty lady who he thinks mistakenly left a briefcase at the airport.

Of course, Mary has left the briefcase in the terminal deliberately. It is filled with cash—ransom money to meet the demands of her husband's kidnappers. Lloyd and Harry don't know this, nor do they know what's in the briefcase. The film's bad guys naturally know about the cash, however, and they desperately want to get it back. They chase the two nitwits across the country.

Added to this is the fact that Harry is driving his business's "Mutts-Cutts" truck—not a difficult vehicle to spot on the road or parked at a diner. The truck has been customized to resemble a gigantic furry dog at great expense to Harry, who is himself outfitted in a floppy-eared doggie costume in an attempt to keep his job. Unfortunately, Harry loses the job delivering show animals to dog trials because of his bad driving and his tendency to feed the dogs en route to the contests.

Lloyd's lot is no better. He loses his most recent job as a limousine driver when he leaves the scene of an accident he has caused in his attempt to catch Mary at the airport. To Lloyd and Harry, staying in the dismal apartment they share really doesn't make any more sense than driving halfway across the country to Aspen, Colorado, to deliver the briefcase to Mary.

Dumb and Dumber doesn't pretend to be highbrow entertainment. Its title pretty much describes the two main characters—and the plot line as well. But the process of making the film was anything but dumb. The movie's tar-

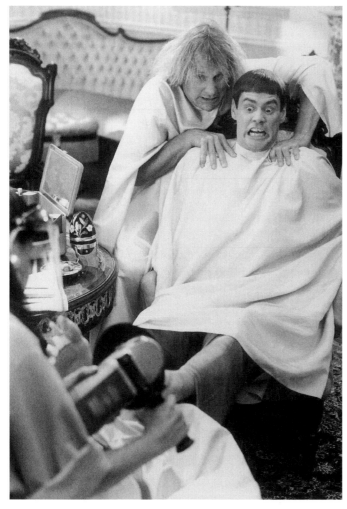

Harry Dunn (Jeff Daniels) watches as Lloyd Christmas (Carrey) receives a pedicure in the 1994 movie Dumb and Dumber.

get audience was adolescent boys, and it hit its mark: *Dumb and Dumber* scored a bull's-eye with that group. After the film's release during the 1994 holiday season, Jim Carrey would have a third hit on his hands.

After Carrey finished work on *Dumb and Dumber*, he was scheduled to appear on several talk shows to promote *The Mask*, which was about to be released. Every actor who stars in a movie is expected to make such appearances to talk about his or her new movie and perhaps to introduce a "clip" from the film—a tiny bit of the movie that is

Jim Carrey with his future wife, Lauren Holly, in Dumb and Dumber.

supposed to entice the show's viewers to see the film. This routine is one of the best ways to let people know what the new movie is about.

Jim knew that it was important to make as many television appearances as possible. But he had a slight problem. His doctors told him that he had to have surgery first. Jim Carrey had no choice; his gallbladder had to be removed. Amazingly he managed to squeeze in the operation during early June 1994.

Fortunately the surgery went off without a hitch, and the patient apparently kept his odd sense of humor throughout the ordeal. Wayne Flemming, who came to see his longtime friend during his hospital stay, spoke to the press right after the operation was over. He wanted people to know just how funny Jim Carrey really is. According to Flemming, as the sedated Carrey was wheeled out of surgery, he began pretending that he was driving the gurney by making the noises and motions of shifting gears in a car.

He undoubtedly had help from the hospital staff, but Jim Carrey managed to make the trip back to his hospital room safely—sound effects and all. He recovered from his operation in time to make his talk-show appearances for *The Mask*, and his speedy recovery also allowed him to attend the premiere of the film on July 29, 1994.

Premiere night for a major motion picture can be quite impressive, especially when you happen to be the star of the film. Crowds of fans line up along the sidewalks outside the theater, waiting to catch a glimpse of you as you step out of your limousine. Jim Carrey had a little trouble getting used to all of the sudden fuss. He still felt like a regular guy; he'd just acted in a few movies, that's all. So he felt right at home when something funny happened as he was leaving one of the premieres.

Carrey was trying his best to play the part of the Hollywood star as he left the theater. He walked to his limo. There stood his driver, who had locked the keys in the limousine. The motor was running, and the driver was trying to pick the lock.

Instead of being whisked away from the premiere feeling glamorous and suave, Jim Carrey ended up doing his best to remain undisturbed and laugh at how life has a way of reminding you not to take yourself too seriously.

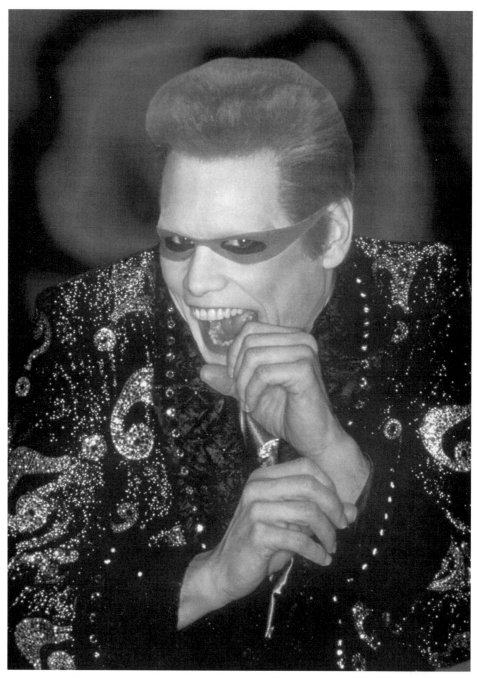

Jim Carrey's elastic facial expressions and limber body served him well in his role as the exuberantly evil Riddler in Batman Forever.

7

BATMAN
AND BEYOND

ACTOR VAL KILMER had never seen *Earth Girls Are Easy* and had never caught an episode of *In Living Color*. But as he prepared for his title role in the film *Batman Forever*, he was naturally curious about the man who would be playing his archenemy. Yet he knew nothing about Jim Carrey's work. He decided he needed to see something that Jim had done, so he watched *Ace Ventura, Pet Detective*. Kilmer only had to see the opening scene, in which Ace deliberately manhandles a package and pulverizes its contents, before he was on the phone calling the studio to voice his approval of his *Batman* costar. He already knew that filming *Batman Forever* with Carrey as the Riddler would be great fun.

Kilmer had expected to work with the comic actor Robin Williams, who had long been slated to play the Riddler. But Williams wanted changes made to the script before he would agree to do the picture, and the concept of the film had already been reworked once. Director Joel Schumacher was anxious to get started, so he called Carrey to do the part instead. Having finished a phenomenal year at the box office, Jim Carrey would make this third film in the Batman series even more bankable than its predecessors. Robin Williams was out. Jim Carrey was in.

Indeed, as in *The Mask*, Carrey seemed perfect for the role. Moviegoers were once again treated to Carrey's fluid face and dynamic body movements. And once again, Carrey donned a costume that was custom-made to emphasize his character's personality.

Without a doubt, the colorful Carrey brightens the otherwise dark and ominous set depicting the fictional Gotham City. While the other characters dress in black, the Riddler stands out in a garishly green, skintight bodysuit festooned with printed question marks. The Riddler's hair, too, is exceedingly colorful—a sort of "Bozo the Clown meets the buzz cut" style. Carrey briefly entertained the idea of taking the hairstyle even further. He had seen how athletes shave initials and numbers into their hair. What if he shaved a gigantic question mark into the top of his hair, forming the bottom of the question mark out of the hair at the nape of his neck? Wouldn't that really set off the Riddler?

Maybe it would have been the definitive "do" for the *Batman* character, but Jim had to consider his coiffure for upcoming ventures as well. Suppose the hair didn't grow back in time for him to film the sequel to *Ace Ventura*? After all, Ace just wouldn't be Ace without his gravity-defying hair. More importantly, what if remnants of the question mark remained emblazoned on his scalp when he went before the judge during his upcoming divorce proceedings with Melissa Womer?

Jim joked in later interviews that such a hairdo would suggest that he was "questioning the judge's judgment." Although the remark was made in jest, the pending divorce was on Carrey's mind. He may have joked about the hairdo, but one thing was certain—he did not want to do anything that would jeopardize his chance of being awarded joint custody of his daughter, Jane.

The divorce proceedings took place in August 1995,

and Melissa and Jim agreed to share the custody of their daughter. Although shooting on location sometimes takes Carrey away from home for long periods—and Jane can't always accompany him because of her school schedule— father and daughter still try to spend as much time together as they can.

Carrey's dual role in *The Mask* supplied a springboard from which to launch another such character for the Batman project. Once again, Carrey plays not one but two roles: he begins as an inventor named Edward Nygma, who works by day for Batman alter ego Bruce Wayne. Nygma toils after hours in the electronic division of Wayne's company, perfecting a brain-altering 3-D TV device in an effort to impress his employer, whom he greatly admires. But when Wayne turns down the idea because he believes it is immoral to attempt to control the human brain, Nygma is devastated. His idol has rejected his life's work! Ultimately, Nygma seeks what every wronged comic-book character wishes for—revenge!

The two villains of Batman Forever—*Harvey "Two Face" Dent (Tommy Lee Jones) and the Riddler (Jim Carrey)—plot revenge on the movie's superhero.*

Without a doubt, Carrey's Riddler earns every question mark that peppers his costume. His voice, his mannerisms, and his riddling remarks are all in keeping with his Riddler persona. And Carrey's own elasticized movements, as he curves and contorts his entire body, suggest a life-sized human question mark.

Most moviegoers and critics seemed to agree that Carrey's tour de force performance is so energized, so dynamic, that he steals the show. Not that this was an easy task: for starters, there was much pre-film publicity about the "new" Batman, Val Kilmer, who replaced the former Batman, Michael Keaton, for this third installment. In addition, the comic-book character's faithful sidekick, Robin, played by Chris O'Donnell, was introduced in *Batman Forever*. And the Riddler is not the only villain in the movie. Harvey "Two Face" Dent is also out to foil Batman and Robin as they go about protecting Gotham City's residents. Both sides of the evil Dent are portrayed by one of Hollywood's favorite heavies, Tommy Lee Jones, in a powerful performance. His Dent is menacing and decidedly evil, but the Riddler had audiences buzzing as they left the theaters.

People mainly wanted to know how Carrey could possibly move his body in the ways he did. Just as he had impressed and amazed *Mask* fans, Carrey again wowed filmgoers with his incredible flexibility. But it was more than a physical stretch that Carrey had undertaken in playing the Riddler. He was playing a completely different kind of character from earlier roles—this time, he was a gleeful villain. The comedian from Canada was once more displaying his broad range on the big screen.

With *Batman* under his belt, Carrey began working on still another project. But this time his work would not involve a new character: he signed on to reprise his role as a pet detective in a sequel called *Ace Ventura: When Nature Calls*. This time, instead of tracking down a dolphin, the self-proclaimed world's best—and still only—

pet detective was hot on the trail of an albino bat.

His costar for the new movie was British actor Ian McNeice. McNeice had never seen the first *Ace Ventura* picture until his agent called to tell him about a possible role in a sequel. McNeice decided he had better catch up on his film viewing. He watched a videotape of *Pet Detective* with his two children, then aged 10 and 11. His kids loved the movie, and they couldn't believe that their dad had a chance to work with someone as funny as Jim Carrey. No acting job their father had ever done seemed as important. Dad was going to work with the one and only Jim Carrey!

McNeice's children weren't the only ones who were excited about the sequel. Carrey himself was anxious to revisit the character he had brought to life the previous year. He set about trying to out-ace Ace.

As the studio began production, however, it became apparent that problems were developing on the set. The wonderful working relationship Carrey had had on *Pet Detective* with director Tom Shadyac was missing. Carrey did not enjoy the same rapport with *Nature*'s director, Tom

Reprising his role as the world's only pet detective in the 1995 movie Ace Ventura: When Nature Calls, *Jim Carrey mugs for the camera and his animal costars.*

DeChercio. Tempers flared, causing model-turned-actress Georgianna Robertson to quit after just one day of work.

The option of quitting wasn't available to Carrey, however. He was the star of the film, and it wouldn't work without him. After all, the movie would never have been considered had it not been for Carrey's wildly successful first role. Unlike the series of Batman films, where the title role could easily be filled by a replacement, this character had been custom-made for Carrey. He was the only one who could play Ace—and there was no mask behind which he could hide.

Unfortunately, Carrey did feel like quitting. He and DeChercio just could not work together. They didn't have the creative give-and-take that Carrey had had with Shadyac. Instead, the relationship was filled with tension, anger, and many discussions that turned into arguments. Carrey couldn't quit, but he could bring production to a screeching halt if he didn't show up on the set. Which is exactly what he finally did.

Jim Carrey didn't know how long it would take for the studio to get the message that he was not happy, but he didn't care. He holed himself up in his studio trailer and vowed that he wouldn't come out until something was done about the situation.

Tom DeChercio was fired.

Steve Oedekerk was hired to replace him. He and Jim were good friends who had worked together in television. Oedekerk had been a writer for *In Living Color* when Jim was on the show. In many ways, bringing Oedekerk and Carrey together again was good. They were used to working with one another and fell into an easy rhythm. However, that may have allowed the two to fall back into the ways of filming for television, where there is little time to perfect scenes and dialogue. As a result, much of the *Ace Ventura* sequel seems to rely on jokes that stand alone fairly well but have little to do with the scenes that follow. While that method may work well for a TV variety show, it ends up confusing an audience trying to follow the plot line of a movie.

Although Carrey and Oedekerk worked to revive Ace's character, the damage had been done. The movie was modestly successful at the box office, but a great deal of its success depended on the popularity of the original Ace picture. People had returned to the theater to see what Ace Ventura was up to, but many left feeling disappointed.

Ace Ventura is clearly a one-of-a-kind, zany genius, and audiences loved him in *Pet Detective*. In the sequel, however, much of what Ace says and does is just plain gross. The title should have tipped off moviegoers: "when nature calls" is a polite way of describing going to the bathroom. In this film, it also means that Ace works mostly in the wild, with nature as a backdrop. Nevertheless, a good deal of the humor has to do with bathroom jokes. Adolescents seemed to enjoy this kind of humor, but more mature viewers weren't impressed.

Some filmgoers were offended not only by the base humor but also by the depiction of natives in the film. There's a good reason that ethnic tribal dances and rituals are no longer trivialized on film the way they once were. Modern audiences no longer accept stereotyped versions of ethnic groups—no matter where those groups live. It just isn't funny to ridicule the religious beliefs or customs of another culture. These days, most people strive to be "politically correct," which means that they try their best not to say or do anything to offend a person of another race, belief, or culture. Often remarks or actions that play on stereotypes are not only offensive, but they also make those who hear them uncomfortable. And it's hard for most people to laugh when they feel uncomfortable.

Perhaps for similar reasons, audiences were also ill at ease watching Jim Carrey in his 1996 movie, *The Cable Guy*. Carrey plays a cable TV installer and repairman named Ernie Douglas, who grew up with only television shows for company.

"The old TV was always there for me," Jim Carrey's lonely, quirky character claimed in the 1996 movie The Cable Guy.

Carrey's cable guy is a product of many hours of TV-watching. At various times, the cable guy calls himself either Ernie or Chip, adopting the names of two characters from a popular and long-running television show called *My Three Sons*: Ernie and Chip were two of the three Douglas sons. Stevie, played by Matthew Broderick, knows exactly where the names came from and begins to wonder about this cable guy.

Both Carrey and director Ben Stiller are members of what has been called the "TV generation"—those who grew up when television was still a relatively new contraption and watched it so much that it was often called the "electronic babysitter." Parents discovered that they could plunk their kids in front of the TV for hours at a time and know that they were safe and entertained. The cable guy reflects this when he describes his own childhood: "When I was a kid, my mom worked nights. I never met my father. But the old TV was always there for me."

Stiller's parents were the television comedy team

known as Stiller and Meara, so Ben grew up not only watching TV shows, but also seeing how they were made. Audiences may see in the movie's ending Stiller's assessment of what happens when kids spend too much time in front of the TV. Carrey's character knocks out every home's satellite signal in an attempt to "kill the babysitter." He is performing a twisted sort of public service, claiming that although it is too late for him, "there are lots of little cable boys and girls out there who still have a chance."

Today's audiences often do not feel right about making fun of other people's faults or differences if they are not correctable. Most of us would find it perfectly acceptable to laugh at a person who acts out of character—for example, a young boy who has fallen in love and is so busy thinking about the girl he likes that he puts the milk carton in the cupboard and the cereal box in the refrigerator. In this case, it's amusing to think that falling in love can make a perfectly reasonable person do something unreasonable. However, we might find it sad, or even tragic, if the person making this mistake were a victim of Alzheimer's disease or another debilitating affliction.

Audiences are never sure exactly which of these two types of people the cable guy really is. At times, he appears to be merely a harmless but strange friend to Stevie. At other times, he seems menacing or disturbed, someone who has a mental disability or whom Stevie should fear. For this reason, the film never achieved the success of many of Carrey's previous movies.

If director Ben Stiller had a deep, dark message to relay to moviegoers, Carrey brought something even darker to the film. When Ernie isn't installing cable he is watching it from his van. His life may revolve around the seemingly limitless world of television, but he lives in a very small place—the van—just as Jim and his family had when Percy Carrey lost his job. Perhaps the sad little cable guy was a little too real to the actor who played him.

Carrey jokes with reporters during a press conference in Germany promoting the release of the 1997 movie Liar, Liar.

8

HONESTY IS THE BEST POLICY

TRUTH BE TOLD, Jim Carrey needed a good, solid movie after *The Cable Guy* and *Ace Ventura: When Nature Calls*. Both movies had been disappointing at the box office. Carrey's next film, *Liar, Liar,* seemed to be just what his movie career needed.

Produced by Universal Studios, the project once again paired Carrey with director Tom Shadyac, who had worked with Carrey on the first *Ace Ventura* picture. No one would ever confuse Carrey with his childhood hero, actor Jimmy Stewart, but as attorney Fletcher Reede in *Liar, Liar,* Carrey was an honest-to-goodness leading man.

He certainly looked the part in the movie. Reede is well-heeled and downright handsome. True, he can hardly be considered a traditional matinee idol during the film's outrageous courtroom scenes, in which he manages to make a mockery of the legal profession and a bruised, battered, disheveled mess of himself. But during most of the movie Jim is decked out in the tailored dress of a high-priced lawyer, eager to become partner in a prestigious law firm. In this movie, Carrey wears $400 suits, not the tropical shirts and striped trousers favored by Ace

77

Ventura or the bright-green Riddler suit he donned for *Batman Forever*. Nor does Carrey sport a pastel tuxedo like the one he wore for *Dumb and Dumber* or the fetching red space suit of *Earth Girls are Easy*. Perhaps there is truth after all in the old adage, "Clothes make the man."

Carrey's bad hair days appear to be behind him as well. In *Liar, Liar*, Fletcher Reede's hair does not defy gravity à la Ace Ventura, nor is it dyed orange as the Riddler's was. It's not even cropped in a bowl cut like that of Lloyd Christmas. Fletcher Reede's hair is painstakingly normal—leading-man normal.

But looks aren't everything. Reede's behavior is also noticeably different from that of Carrey's other characters. Perhaps most important, Reede appears to have attended a different driver's education class than most of the other characters Carrey has played. In a departure from Ace Ventura's head-out-the-window technique, Reede drives almost sedately, with his head safely behind a windshield that hasn't been shattered by a bad guy's baseball bat or his own deliberately violent parking methods. Moreover, he steers with his hands and not his feet. Carrey has clearly come a long way with his on-screen driving skills—although Fletcher Reede does drive a little recklessly when he is in a hurry. Ironically, Reede is also the first of Carrey's characters who is actually reprimanded for driving erratically. He is pulled over for reckless driving by a police officer, who impounds Reede's car because of a glove box full of unpaid parking tickets.

Fletcher Reede is the most realistic of Carrey's screen characters, and he is also the only one who obeys the law. By contrast, Ace Ventura's flamboyant style places him above the law—and in fact, he is better at sleuthwork than many members of the police department. The mild-mannered Stanley Ipkiss does no wrong—it's his alter ego, the Mask, who robs a bank and steals the girl. In the cartoon city of Gotham, the Riddler's run-in with the law comes in the form of a duel with a masked crusader, not a con-

frontation with a uniformed police officer. And some form of intergalactic diplomatic immunity must shelter the alien Wiploc from the law, or he would quickly be arrested for his way-out, spacey driving.

Attorney Fletcher Reede lives in the fast-paced '90s, with all the trappings of a modern-day man, including a son, Max (portrayed by Justin Cooper), and an ex-wife, Audrey (played by Maura Tierney). Lying is a way of life for Reede. The self-absorbed lawyer believes himself too busy even to take office calls from his own mother. Instead, he has his secretary screen calls and offer Mom and anyone else with whom he doesn't wish to talk a running list of acceptable, if not entirely believable, excuses. As the stereotypical unethical lawyer, he routinely represents criminals and gets them off scot-free. He's too busy trying to advance his career to feel the least bit of conflict, not only over helping criminals win their free-

The well-meaning but dishonest dad Fletcher Reede (Jim Carrey) tries to convince his son, Max (Justin Cooper), to reverse his birthday wish in Liar, Liar.

Jim Carrey's devotion to his daughter, Jane, is evident as he imprints his hands and feet in the "walk of fame" at Hollywood's Mann's Chinese Theater.

dom, but also for demanding that their victims pay damages to his clients.

Sadly, Reede is also too busy to remember his own son's birthday. His big-hearted secretary bails him out by buying and wrapping an appropriate gift for the boy just in time for the big day. But Dad can't even take a moment to play catch with Max once his new baseball and glove are unwrapped. If Reede remembers to show up at all, he is always late for his outings with Max, who lives in suburbia with his mom, Fletcher's ex-wife. Reede breaks promises regularly.

Max badly wants to believe his father, and each time he is supposed to see him he allows himself to get excited. He doesn't let his father's lousy track record of keeping promises stand in the way. Always hopeful that Dad will change, the young boy sets himself up for one disappointment after another.

When it's time to cut the cake at his birthday party, Max is one disappointed birthday boy. The cake, the party-goers, the balloons, and even the hired clown don't matter to Max. His father isn't there. Max wants to continue to wait for his dad, but Mom convinces him not to. Resigned to the fact that his father is not going to make it to his birthday party, Max makes a wish as he finally blows out the candles. It's a desperate wish, and even Max doesn't believe it will ever come true, although it's something that he wants more than anything in the whole world. He wishes that—for just one day—his father cannot tell a lie.

Max's whimsical wish becomes the focus of the entire movie. As Hollywood would have it, his wish comes true. As the smoke from the cake's candles wafts through the window, Fletcher Reede becomes completely incapable of telling a lie. The movie's premise provides Jim Carrey with a marvelous opportunity for verbal and physical comedy. He's a lawyer to whom lying is a way of life, who is suddenly unable even to fib just a little. He's forced to be brutally honest about everything. He cannot even utter the day-to-day "little white lies" that most people tell out of politeness: he can't see a person's bad hairdo or weight problem or annoying habit without commenting on it. He is now compelled to state the truth—no matter how hurtful it may be. Of course, the predicament in which Fletcher finds himself causes all sorts of problems.

Through a conversation with Audrey, Fletcher comes to understand how he wound up in this situation. He immediately attempts to find a solution by paying a visit to Max at school. While the class is in recess, Max talks to his dad and discovers that his wish has come true. He's still marveling at his luck when his dad, who believes that Max can undo the wish, produces a second birthday cake and a pair of party hats. Max agrees to make a second wish, but before he does, he makes Fletcher truthfully answer a laundry list of questions.

One of Max's questions is whether a child's face will really "freeze" if he makes a funny face too often. Many of us have probably heard this as children, and Jim Carrey heard a variation of it while he was growing up. Jim's mother, desperate to get her son to stop making faces in the mirror, once told him that if he looked too long into the mirror he would see the devil. As Jim tells the story, it was the wrong thing to say. For one thing, it only made him curious about what the devil looked like; for another, if the devil did show himself, Jim figured that perhaps the two of them could work out some sort of deal.

With that in mind, Carrey's Fletcher Reede truthfully answers Max's question—no, he says, your face won't freeze. But Carrey couldn't resist commenting that some people make very good money making funny faces.

The line gets a big laugh from moviegoers, but in this scene the last laugh belongs to Max. Much as he'd like to please his father, he just can't undo his birthday wish. Fletcher's predicament remains unchanged. He still cannot tell a lie, and his attempts to stretch the truth continue to be extremely comical.

But this hilarious situation is tempered by seriousness. Forced to represent an unscrupulous client in court on a day when he has promised to visit Max, Fletcher faces losing his son entirely. Max's mother has watched their son endure all the broken promises he can bear and is about to move Max away from his father and the constant heartbreak and disappointment. This visit may be Reede's last chance to make amends.

Although Reede actually has a legitimate excuse, no excuse is going to be good enough this time. He has run out of chances. In being honest with himself, he realizes that even though he loves his boy dearly, he has been a bad father.

Fletcher's madcap, last-minute race to reach Max is full of the antics that moviegoers have come to expect from Carrey. His face and his body contort every which way. But this time, Carrey's physical comedy is part of a realistic character whose efforts to get to Max are hilariously silly, but whose reasons for wanting to see his son are not. Reede wants Max to know that he loves him and that he will do absolutely anything to restore Max's trust in him.

In some ways, Fletcher Reede is similar to Jim Carrey. Both are divorced dads. Carrey's daughter, Jane, is very important to him. His filming schedule is often long and arduous, and Jim must feel as though he has to pull off moves similar to those of Fletcher Reede to see his daughter. But like any parent, famous or unknown, Jim Carrey the dad endures this "juggling act" willingly because of his love for Jane.

Fans sometimes do not understand when Jim Carrey wants to spend time alone with his daughter. Those who see him on the street or at a restaurant nearly always ask him to sign an autograph or make one of his patented funny faces. Most times, Jim will gladly oblige his fans, even taking a moment to chat with them. There are times, however, when Jim Carrey just wants to be Jane's dad. He wants her to know that all of his attention is focused on her. That's because out of all his many roles, Carrey takes that of Dad most seriously.

Carrey and his second wife, Lauren Holly, in 1996. The two had met two years earlier as costars in the movie Dumb and Dumber. *Although Carrey and Holly divorced in 1997, they remain on good terms with one another.*

9

A FISH
CALLED JIM

BEING FAMOUS HAS its drawbacks. Carrey's face is so easily rec-
ognizable that it's difficult for him to appear in public unnoticed. For
example, when he and his second wife, Lauren Holly, tried to spend
some time together on the West Indies island of Antigua during their
honeymoon, they encountered some persistent—and rude—fans. One
tourist thought he could make a handsome profit from a videotape of
the famous couple. He persisted in taping the newlyweds, even after
they requested several times that he stop. Carrey finally called the local
police, and the would-be moviemaker was arrested, but not until after
a scene had taken place. Jim Carrey and Lauren Holly had hoped to
avoid publicity altogether by asking the man to stop videotaping;
instead, the incident was reported in the papers, and rumors about what
had actually happened swirled around them.

Such is the life of a celebrity. The demands of the public often force
an entertainer's private life into the limelight. Columnists craving juicy
gossip try to find any available tidbit of information regarding the stars
and their loved ones. Jim Carrey and Lauren Holly were no exception.

To make matters worse, many members of the media focused on the failures of the Holly-Carrey match almost as soon as the two actors married late in 1996.

While a happy Jim Carrey gushed about his newfound happiness and showed obvious affection for his new bride, the tabloids made much of the prenuptial agreement that the couple signed before they exchanged vows. The fact is that neither bride nor groom was a stranger to divorce proceedings and alimony payments, and both wanted to have things in writing this time, to avoid any confusion or bitter battles should their marriage not work out.

As it happened, Jim Carrey and Lauren Holly's marriage lasted only 10 months. They separated on July 25, 1997, and Lauren filed for divorce, citing irreconcilable differences. Carrey and Holly have both said that they wish each other only the best.

Carrey's marriage did not work out, but he has had continued success at the box office. *Liar, Liar* was the first film of 1997 to top the $100-million mark, and it did so in just three weeks. Jim Carrey had another hit on his hands. Because fans were reacting favorably to Carrey as a realistic screen character, he decided to explore an even more serious role in *The Truman Show*, due to be released in the summer of 1998. According to Carrey, this is his first truly dramatic film role. But moviegoers should not expect this character, or any of the characters Carrey portrays in the future, to be completely serious. Carrey has never cared for films that don't include some humor, and he hopes to inject some comedy into every role he takes.

In *The Truman Show*, Carrey portrays an insurance adjuster who discovers that his entire life and everyone in it are all part of a hit television show. His life is being broadcast as he lives it. The other characters are aware of this fact long before Truman himself finds out.

As bizarre as the premise sounds, the filming of *The Truman Show* has become even more so. Cast member Dennis Hopper lasted only one day on the set before he

was fired over creative differences with the film's director, Peter Weir. In March 1997 Hopper was replaced by Ed Harris, who plays a television network executive who makes life difficult for Truman.

That same month, while on location in Seaside, Florida, the entire cast and crew, including Carrey, Laura Linney, Noah Emmerich, Brian Delate, Holland Taylor, Harry Shearer, and Natascha McElhone, were exposed to hepatitis A, an infectious disease that is usually transmitted in contaminated food and water. In an effort to contain the spread of the disease, more than 100 cast members received precautionary shots of gamma globulin, a solution of blood protein that provides immunity.

In addition to *The Truman Show*, Jim Carrey has many other projects in the works. He is scheduled to play the title role in a remake of the 1947 film *The Secret Life of Walter Mitty*. The original movie, based on a story by humorist James Thurber, was produced by the legendary Samuel Goldwyn (the "G" in the MGM Studios name); the remake will be produced by Goldwyn's son, Samuel

Among Carrey's upcoming projects is the title role in a remake of the 1947 comedy The Secret Life of Walter Mitty, *which starred Danny Kaye as Mitty.*

Although Carrey has never won an Oscar himself, he agreeably made one of his trademark faces while announcing an award at the 69th annual Academy Awards ceremony in March 1997.

Jr., and directed by Ron Howard. Lowell Ganz and Babaloo Mandel, known for such blockbusters as *City Slickers*, *Splash!*, and *Nightshift*, are writing the new Mitty movie, tentatively scheduled for a Christmas 1998 release.

Another remake may be in the works as well—a modernization of Don Knotts's 1964 movie, *The Incredible Mr. Limpet*, which will rely to a great extent on animation. Mr. Limpet, a weakling with aquatic aspirations, dreams of becoming a fish—and then magically becomes one. Rather than acting in every scene, Jim will do voiceover for the animated fish, who gets most of the screen time. Jim likes that idea almost as much as he likes the material itself.

Carrey is also planning to put on a very different type of performance by contributing his singing talents to an album by ex-Beatles producer George Martin, tentatively titled *In My Life*. Several other celebrities, including Goldie Hawn and Sean Connery, are reportedly lending their voices to the project. Carrey will sing the popular Beatles tune "I Am the Walrus."

This is not Carrey's first venture into the music world. He enjoys songwriting as a form of recreation and has even contributed to a song entitled "Heaven Down Here," recorded by performers Tuck and Patti and released on their album *Learning to Fly*. Carrey penned the love ballad with his friend Phil Roy.

Whether or not all of these planned projects are realized, Jim Carrey is going to return to the big screen. In 1994 he signed a $10-million contract for a sequel to *The Mask*, called *Revenge of the Mask*; however, both Carrey and the director, Charles Russell, are busy with other projects and the film has been put on hold. There is also talk of a second *Dumb and Dumber* movie, and the Riddler may once again terrorize the streets of Gotham City.

Jim Carrey is a very gifted entertainer with a wide range of interests and talents. He will very likely create other wild and likable characters and complete many more box-office hits. But his style is not for everyone. No doubt he will also work on projects that critics, fans, or even Carrey himself will consider unsuccessful. But Carrey has faced failure before, and he doesn't seem the least bit afraid to face it again. After all, he is his father's son. Percy Carrey was a survivor who was always willing to try again, no matter what life handed him. His son is no different. Percy Carrey was not a quitter, and neither is his son.

Jim Carrey has learned a great deal from his difficult childhood and his early struggles on the stand-up comedy circuits of Canada and America. His father proved to him that perseverance pays off. Or, as Jim puts it, "Failure taught me that failure isn't the end, unless you give up."

APPENDIX

FACTS ABOUT THE HOMELESS IN AMERICA

Jim Carrey and his family were only six of the millions of North Americans who have been homeless at one time or another. People usually become homeless for one of three reasons. They may be displaced from their homes by natural or man-made disasters, such as hurricanes and fires. Or, like the Carreys, they may lose their home or possessions through family breakups, abuse, or loss of a job. Runaway or "throwaway" children and abused women and children are also included in this group. These people often have difficulty resettling permanently. The third and smallest group consists of those who are chronically homeless—that is, those who remain so for long periods of time. The people in this group are more likely to suffer from substance abuse or mental illness.

Many of us think that we know who homeless people are: male adults who are either mentally ill or have drug and alcohol problems, who don't work and don't want to, who are uneducated, or who live in major cities. In fact, according to statistics, these assumptions are true for only a fraction of America's homeless. Here are some facts about the homeless in the United States:

- The average age of a homeless person in America is nine.**
- Families with young children are the fastest-growing segment of the homeless population, making up 40% of people who become homeless.++
- Children account for about 24% of the urban homeless population.++
- The typical homeless family is a single, 20-year-old mother with one or two children under the age of six.**
- Twenty-five to 50% of homeless women and children are fleeing abuse.+
- Over half of all homeless children have never lived in their own home.
- Over 40% have been homeless more than once.**
- About 30% of homeless adults have full- or part-time jobs.* (In many areas of the country, a person who works full-time at a minimum-wage job is at risk for homelessness because his or her pay often cannot cover the cost of housing.)
- Many homeless people have completed high school; some have attended college or graduate school.*

- Forty percent of homeless men have served in the armed forces (compared to 34% of the general adult male population).+
- The ethnic makeup of homeless populations varies according to geographic location. In major cities, for example, 57% are African American, 30% are white, and 13% are Hispanic, Native American, or Asian.# In rural areas, however, most homeless people are white, and homelessness among Native Americans is more common in these areas.
- About 20 to 25% of the single adult homeless population suffers from some form of mental illness; of these, only 5 to 7% need to be institutionalized.+
- About one in four homeless people are substance abusers; of these, most are also mentally ill.*

Sources:
*   The American Homeless Society, 1996
**   Homes for the Homeless, 1996
+   National Coalition for the Homeless, 1997
++   U.S. Bureau of the Census, 1991
#   U.S. Conference of Mayors Survey, 1996

Habitat for Humanity International
121 Habitat Street
Americus, GA 31709-3498
phone: 800-422-4828
fax: 912-924-0641
e-mail: info@habitat.org

Homes for the Homeless
36 Cooper Square, 6th Floor
New York, NY 10003
phone: 212-529-5252
fax: 212-529-7698
e-mail: hn4061@handsnet.org

**National Alliance to End
Homelessness (formerly the Nat'l.
Citizens Committee for Food
& Shelter)**
1518 K Street N.W., Suite 206
Washington, DC 20005
phone: 202-638-1526
fax: 202-638-4664
e-mail: naeh@ari.net

National Coalition for the Homeless
1621 K Street N.W., Suite 1004
Washington, DC 20006
phone: 202-775-1322
fax: 202-775-1316
e-mail: nch@ari.net

**National Student Campaign Against
Hunger & Homelessness**
Julie Miles, Director
11965 Venice Boulevard, Suite 408
Los Angeles, CA 90066
phone: 800-664-8647, ext. 324
fax: 310-391-0053
e-mail: nscah@aol.com

FINDING OUT MORE ABOUT HOMELESSNESS

BOOKS:

Ackerman, Karen. *The Leaves in October*. New York: Yearling Books, 1993.

Barbour, Karen. *Mr. Bow Tie*. New York: Harcourt Brace Jovanovich, 1991.

Bunting, Eve. *Fly Away Home*. Boston: Houghton Mifflin Company, 1991.

Chalofsky, Margie, et al. *Changing Places: A Kid's View of Shelter Living*. Beltsville, MD: Gryphon House, 1992.

Clifford, Eth. *Never Hit a Ghost with a Baseball Bat*. Illustrated by George Hughes. Boston: Houghton Mifflin Company, 1993.

Disalvo-Ryan, Dyanne. *Uncle Willie and the Soup Kitchen*. New York: William Morrow & Co., Inc., 1990.

Fox, Paula. *Monkey Island*. New York: Orchard Books, 1991.

Hahn, Mary Downing. *December Stillness*. New York: Avon Books, 1988.

Hertenstein, Jane. *Home Is Where We Live: Life in a Shelter Through a Young Girl's Eyes*. Illustrated by Bonnie Lee Groth. Chicago: Cornerstone Press, 1995.

Hubbard, Jim. *Lives Turned Upside Down: Homeless Children in Their Own Words and Photographs*. New York: Simon & Schuster, 1996.

Kroll, Virginia L. *Shelter Folks*. Illustrated by Jan Naimo Jones. Grand Rapids, MI: Wm. B. Eerdmans Publishing Company, 1995.

Kroloff, Charles A. *54 Ways You Can Help the Homeless*. New York: Levin Associates, 1993.

London, Jonathan. *Where's Home?* New York: Puffin Books, 1997.

Luger, Harriett. *Bye, Bye, Bali Kai*. New York: Browndeer Press, 1996.

Mazer, Harry. *Cave Under the City*. New York: HarperCollins, 1986.

McGovern, Ann. *The Lady in the Box*. Illustrated by Marni Backer. New York: Turtle Books, 1997.

Mountbatten-Windsor York (Ferguson), Sarah. *Bright Lights*. Illustrated by Jacqueline Rogers. New York: Bantam Books, 1997.

Myers, Bill, and Robert West. *Beauty in the Least*. Wheaton, IL: Tyndale House Publishers, 1993.

Myers, Walter Dean. *Darnell Rock Reporting*. New York: Yearling Books, 1996.

Neufeld, John. *Almost a Hero*. New York: Aladdin Paperbacks, 1996.

Rozakis, Laurie. Homelessness: *Can We Solve the Problem?* Edited by Jeanne

Vestal. Chicago: Twenty First Century Books, 1995.

Sendak, Maurice. *We Are All in the Dumps with Jack and Guy*. New York: Harper-Collins, 1993.

Snyder, Zilpha Keatley. *The Gypsy Game*. New York: Delacorte Press, 1997.

Stewart, Gail B. *The Homeless*. San Diego: Lucent Books, 1996.

VIDEOS:

Don't Make Me Choose. Color/b & w, no date. Produced by Night Vision Productions. Music by Lorrie "Wes" Wesoly. 17 min. Night Vision Productions.

Home Less Home. Color, 1991. 70 min. Bill Brand Productions.

The Homeless Home Movie. Color, 1997. Produced and directed by Pat Hennessey. 84 min. Media Visions.

Rewind: It Could Have Been Me. B & w, no date. Produced, directed, and animated by Lorie Loeb. Music by Holly Near. 13 min. Morning Glory Films.

Survivors of the Streets: Success Stories of Four Who Were Homeless. Color, no date. Produced by Charlann Slater. 28 min. Full Circle Productions.

WEBSITES:

The American Homeless Society Presents Homeless Shelters in the United States
http://www.nmc.edu/~lanninl/us.htm

The Homeless Art Project
http://www.floaters.org/index1.html

Homeless People and the Internet
http://members.tripod.com/~bmdavidson/index.html

Homeless Peoples Network
http://aspin.asu.edu/hpn/

Kids Helping Kids
http://www.geocities.com/Heartland/8677/

North American Street Newspaper Association
http://www.speakeasy.org/nasna

CHRONOLOGY

1962   Jim Carrey born on January 17 in Newmarket, Ontario

1975   Father Percy Carrey loses his job; the Carrey family moves into factory housing in Scarborough, Ontario

1977   Performs stand-up comedy for the first time at the Yuk Yuk Comedy Club in Toronto

1978   Percy Carrey quits his job; the Carreys are homeless for the next two years

1979   Performs stand-up comedy in Toronto area clubs; makes an appearance at Mitzi Shore's Comedy Store in Los Angeles, California

1981   Tours the comedy club circuit in the United States; becomes a regular at the Comedy Store

1982   Begins opening regularly for Rodney Dangerfield in Las Vegas, Nevada

1984   Stars in the short-lived TV series *The Duck Factory*; lands first film role in *Finders Keepers*

1987   Marries Melissa Womer; daughter Jane is born

1990   Joins the cast of *In Living Color*

1994   Stars in his first hit movie, *Ace Ventura, Pet Detective*; also stars in *The Mask* and *Dumb and Dumber*

1995   Appears in *Batman Forever* and *Ace Ventura: When Nature Calls;* divorces Melissa Womer; Percy Carrey dies

1996   Stars in *The Cable Guy*; marries actress Lauren Holly

1997   Stars in *Liar, Liar*; divorces Lauren Holly

1998   Scheduled to appear in *The Truman Show* and *The Secret Life of Walter Mitty*

Carrey as the outlandish pet detective in the 1995 movie Ace Ventura: When Nature Calls.

FILMOGRAPHY

Finders Keepers (1984)

Once Bitten (1985)

Peggy Sue Got Married (1986)

The Dead Pool (1988)

High Strung (uncredited cameo, 1989)

Earth Girls Are Easy (1989)

Pink Cadillac (1989)

Ace Ventura, Pet Detective (1994)

The Mask (1994)

Dumb and Dumber (1994)

Batman Forever (1995)

Ace Ventura: When Nature Calls (1995)

The Cable Guy (1996)

Liar, Liar (1997)

The Truman Show (scheduled for release 1998)

The Secret Life of Walter Mitty (scheduled for release 1998)

FURTHER READING

Bibby, Bruce. "Riddle Me This, Batman." *Premiere*, May 1995.

Bruno, Mary. "Jim Carrey is God . . . for Now." *Mr. Showbiz Archive News* (Internet), 13 November 1995.

Brunt, Frank. "Jim Carrey, The Man of Silly Faces." *Detroit Free Press*, 14 September 1994.

Giles, Jeff. "Funny Face." *Newsweek*, 26 June 1995.

Hamilton, Kendall, and Carey Monserrate. "It's Not Quite 'Remains of the Day.'" *Newsweek*, 21 February 1994.

Burcham, Becky. "Jim Carrey Un-Masked!" *Nickelodeon Magazine*, February/March 1995.

Hedegaard, Erik. "Nobody's Fool." *Details*, August 1994.

Mr. Showbiz (Internet), "Jim Carrey Set for *Superman*?" *News Review: Hollywood Headlines*, 15 May 1997.

Mr. Showbiz (Internet), "Jim Carrey and Lauren Holly Kaput?" *News Review: Hollywood Headlines*, 16 May 1997.

Mr. Showbiz (Internet), various articles on Jim Carrey, *Star Bios*, 26 August 1996–17 May 1997.

Schruers, Fred. "Jim Carrey." *Rolling Stone*, 13 July, 1995.

Sherrill, Martha. "Renaissance Man." *Esquire*, December 1995.

Siegel, Scott and Barbara Siegel. *The Jim Carrey Scrapbook*. New York: Citadel, 1995.

Tucker, Ken. "Lord Jim." *Entertainment Weekly*, 5 August 1994.

Walters, Barbara. Interview with Jim Carrey. *The Barbara Walters Show*, 27 March 1995.

INDEX

PICTURE CREDITS

Mary Hughes graduated from the University of Maryland with a degree in Radio, Television and Film. She enjoyed substitute teaching for many years before tackling her current assignment as a computer lab technician at an elementary school in Maryland. An avid baseball fan, Ms. Hughes writes feature articles about major- and minor-league ballplayers in the Baltimore Orioles organization. She often gets an inside peek at just what it takes to make it to the big leagues and how special it can be to remain there. Her favorite ballplayer is her teenaged son, Mark Hudson. Coincidentally, Mark's favorite actor is Jim Carrey.

James Scott Brady serves on the board of trustees with the Center to Prevent Handgun Violence and is the Vice Chairman of the Brain Injury Foundation. Mr. Brady served as Assistant to the President and White House Press Secretary under President Ronald Reagan. He was severely injured in an assassination attempt on the president, but remained the White House Press Secretary until the end of the administration. Since leaving the White House, Mr. Brady has lobbied for stronger gun laws. In November 1993, President Bill Clinton signed the Brady Bill, a national law requiring a waiting period on handgun purchases and a background check on buyers.